The Maritime Dimension of International Security

Terrorism, Piracy, and Challenges for the United States

Peter Chalk

Prepared for the United States Air Force

Approved for public release; distribution unlimited

PROJECT AIR FORCE

The research described in this report was sponsored by the United States Air Force under Contract FA7014-06-C-0001. Further information may be obtained from the Strategic Planning Division, Directorate of Plans, Hq USAF.

Library of Congress Cataloging-in-Publication Data

Chalk, Peter.
    The maritime dimension of international security : terrorism, piracy, and challenges for the United States / Peter Chalk.
        p. cm.
    "The research presented here was sponsored within RAND's Project AirForce (PAF) Strategy and Doctrine Program, as part of a wider effort exploring new concepts for joint U.S. air-naval operations"—Pref.
    Includes bibliographical references.
    ISBN 978-0-8330-4299-6 (pbk. : alk. paper)
    1. Merchant marine—Security measures—United States. 2. Security, International. 3. Shipping—Security measures. 4. Maritime terrorism—Prevention. 5. Terrorism—Prevention. 6. Piracy—Prevention. 7. Unified operations (Military science)—United States. I. Title.

VK203.C48 2008
359'.030973—dc22
                                                                2008014133

The RAND Corporation is a nonprofit research organization providing objective analysis and effective solutions that address the challenges facing the public and private sectors around the world. RAND's publications do not necessarily reflect the opinions of its research clients and sponsors.

Published 2008 by the RAND Corporation
1776 Main Street, P.O. Box 2138, Santa Monica, CA 90407-2138
1200 South Hayes Street, Arlington, VA 22202-5050
4570 Fifth Avenue, Suite 600, Pittsburgh, PA 15213-2665
RAND URL: http://www.rand.org/
To order RAND documents or to obtain additional information, contact
Distribution Services: Telephone: (310) 451-7002;
Fax: (310) 451-6915; Email: order@rand.org

Preface

In today's global environment, transnational security challenges—so-called grey-area phenomena—pose serious and dynamic challenges to national and international stability. These dangers, which cannot be readily defeated by the traditional defenses that states have erected to protect both their territories and populaces, reflect the remarkable fluidity that currently characterizes world politics—a setting in which it is no longer apparent exactly who can do what to whom with what means. The maritime realm is especially conducive to these types of threat contingencies given its vast, largely unregulated, and opaque nature. Two specific issues that have elicited particular attention are piracy and seaborne terrorism. This monograph assesses the nature, scope, and dimensions of these two manifestations of nonstate violence at sea, the extent to which they are or are not interrelated, and their overall relevance to U.S. national and international security interests.

The research presented here was sponsored within the RAND Project AIR FORCE (PAF) Strategy and Doctrine Program as a part of a fiscal year 2006 study, "Exploring New Concepts for Joint Air-Naval Operations." The monograph draws heavily on interviews with maritime experts and intelligence and security analysts who, given the sensitivity of the subject matter, requested that their comments and insights be used on a not-for-attribution basis. Names and affiliated organizations of these individuals have therefore been omitted from the text.

RAND Project AIR FORCE

RAND Project AIR FORCE, a division of the RAND Corporation, is the U.S. Air Force's federally funded research and development center for studies and analyses. PAF provides the Air Force with independent analyses of policy alternatives affecting the development, employment, combat readiness, and support of current and future aerospace forces. Research is conducted in four programs: Aerospace Force Development; Manpower, Personnel, and Training; Resource Management; and Strategy and Doctrine.

Additional information about PAF is available on our Web site: http://www.rand.org/paf/

Contents

Figures

Tables

Summary

Maritime Piracy

Scope and Dimensions

A total of 2,463 actual or attempted acts of piracy were registered around the world between 2000 and the end of 2006. This represents an annual average incident rate of 352, a substantial increase over the mean of 209 recorded for the period of 1994–1999.

The concentration of pirate attacks continues to be greatest in Southeast Asia, especially in the waters around the Indonesian archipelago (including stretches of the Malacca Straits that fall under the territorial jurisdiction of the Jakarta government), which accounted for roughly 25 percent of all global incidents during 2006.

Factors Accounting for the Emergence of Piracy in the Contemporary Era

Seven main factors have contributed to the general emergence of piracy in the contemporary era. First and most fundamentally, there has been a massive increase in commercial maritime traffic. Combined with the large number of ports around the world, this growth has provided pirates with an almost limitless range of tempting, high-payoff targets.

Second is the higher incidence of seaborne commercial traffic that passes through narrow and congested maritime chokepoints. These bottlenecks require ships to significantly reduce speed to ensure safe passage, which dramatically heightens their exposure to midsea interception and attack.

Third, and specifically relevant to Southeast Asia, has been the lingering effects of the Asian financial crisis. Not only did this event exert a stronger "pull factor" on piracy—with more people (including members of the security forces) drawn to maritime and other crime— it also deprived many littoral states of the necessary revenue to fund effective monitoring regimes over their coastlines.

Fourth, the general difficulties associated with maritime surveillance have been significantly heightened as a result of the events of September 11, 2001, and the concomitant pressure that has been exerted on many governments to invest in expensive, land-based homeland security initiatives.

Fifth, lax coastal and port-side security have played an important role in enabling low-level piratical activity, especially harbor thefts of goods from ships at anchor.

Sixth, corruption and emergent voids of judicial prerogative have encouraged official complicity in high-level pirate rings, which has impacted directly on the "phantom ship" phenomenon.[1]

Seventh, the global proliferation of small arms has provided pirates (as well as terrorists and other criminal elements) with an enhanced means to operate on a more destructive and sophisticated level.

The Dangers of Piracy

The dangers associated with contemporary piracy are complex and multifaceted. At the most basic level, attacks constitute a direct threat to the lives and welfare of the citizens of a variety of flag states. Piracy also has a direct economic impact in terms of fraud, stolen cargos, and delayed trips, and could potentially undermine a maritime state's trading ability.

Politically, piracy can play a pivotal role in undermining and weakening regime legitimacy by encouraging corruption among elected government officials. Finally, attacks have the potential to trigger a major environmental disaster, particularly if they take place in crowded sea-lanes traversed by heavily laden oil tankers.

---

[1]   The *phantom ship* phenomenon involves the outright hijacking of oceangoing vessels and their reregistration under flags of convenience for the purposes of illicit trade.

Terrorism

Over the past six years, there has been a modest yet highly discernible spike in high-profile terrorist attacks and plots at sea. These various incidents have galvanized fears in the West that terrorists, especially militants connected with the international jihadist network, are moving to decisively extend operational mandates beyond purely territorially bounded theaters.

Five main factors explain the presumed shift in extremist focus to water-based environments. First, many of the vulnerabilities that have encouraged a higher rate of pirate attacks also apply to terrorism.

Second, the growth of commercial enterprises specializing in maritime sports and equipment has arguably provided terrorists with a readily accessible conduit through which to gain the necessary training and resources for operating at sea.

Third, maritime attacks offer terrorists an alternate means of causing mass economic destabilization. Disrupting the mechanics of the contemporary "just enough, just in time" cargo freight trading system could potentially trigger vast and cascading fiscal effects, especially if the operations of a major commercial port were curtailed.

Fourth, sea-based terrorism constitutes a further means of inflicting mass coercive punishment on enemy audiences. Cruise ships and passenger ferries are especially relevant in this regard because they cater to large numbers of people who are confined in a single physical space.

Finally, the expansive global container-shipping complex offers terrorists a viable logistical conduit for facilitating the covert movement of weapons and personnel in two critical respects. First, because much of the maritime trading system is designed to be as accessible and flexible as possible (to keep costs low and turnover high), there is no strong incentive to enact a stringent (and disruptive) regime of security measures. Second, the highly complex nature of the containerized supply chain, combined with the ineffectiveness of point-of-origin inspections, creates a plethora of openings for terrorist infiltration by providing extremists with numerous opportunities to "stuff" or otherwise tamper with boxed crates.

A Terrorism–Piracy Nexus?

Complicating the maritime threat picture is growing speculation that a tactical nexus could emerge between piracy and terrorism. One of the main concerns is that extremist groups will seek to overcome existing operational constraints in sea-based capabilities by working in conjunction with or subcontracting out missions to maritime crime gangs and syndicates.

The presumed convergence between maritime terrorism and piracy remains highly questionable, however. To date, there has been no credible evidence to support speculation about such a nexus emerging. Just as importantly, the objectives of the two actors remain entirely distinct.

That said, the possibility of a possible conflation between piracy and terrorism has informed the perceptions of governments, international organizations, and major shipping interests around the world. There have been persistent reports of political extremists boarding vessels in Southeast Asia in an apparent effort to learn how to pilot them for a rerun of 9/11 at sea. Indeed, such a specter was a principal factor in driving the Lloyd's Joint War Council to briefly designate the Malacca Straits as an area of enhanced risk in 2005.

Relevance to the United States

The United States has been at the forefront of several moves to upgrade global maritime security over the last five years, including

- the Container Security Initiative
- the International Ship and Port Facility Security (ISPS) Code
- the Proliferation Security Initiative (PSI)
- the Customs-Trade Partnership Against Terrorism.

In addition to these measures, the United States has been instrumental in instituting regional maritime security initiatives and capacity building in areas recognized as vital to U.S. counterterrorism strategy.

On the positive side, these initiatives have helped to lend a degree of transparency to what has hitherto been a highly opaque theater. On the negative side, these programs suffer from three critical shortfalls as presently configured:

- They are limited in scope.
- They are largely directed at strengthening the security "wall" around commercial seaborne traffic, paying scant attention to contingencies that do not involve containerized cargo.
- With particular reference to the ISPS Code, there is still no definitive means of effectively auditing how well extant measures are being implemented by participating states or, indeed, to gauge their overall utility in terms of dock-side security.

Policy Recommendations

At the policy level, there are at least four major contributions that the United States could make to better safeguard the global oceanic environment, including the following: (1) helping to further expand the nascent regime of post-9/11 maritime security; (2) informing the parameters of bilateral and multilateral maritime security collaboration by conducting regular and rigorous threat assessments; (3) assisting with redefining mandates of existing multilateral security and defense arrangements to allow them to play a more effective and inclusive role in countering maritime (and other transnational) threats; and (4) encouraging the commercial maritime industry to make greater use of enabling communication and defensive technologies and accept a greater degree of transparency in its corporate structures.

In more specific terms, U.S. funds and support could be usefully directed at (1) boosting the coastal monitoring and interdiction capabilities of states in areas of strategic maritime importance; (2) actively supporting the International Maritime Bureau's piracy reporting center in Malaysia; (3) augmenting port security management; and (4) sponsoring research into cost-effective initiatives for better securing ships and oceanic freight.

Acknowledgments

The author would like to thank the two reviewers of this monograph—Martin Murphy of the University of Reading, UK, and William Rosenau of the RAND Corporation—for sharing their insights, probing for weaknesses, correcting errors, and helping to improve the overall quality of the analysis. The author would also like to acknowledge the numerous maritime experts and intelligence and security analysts who agreed to be interviewed for the study but who asked not to be identified by name or affiliated organization. Finally, a special debt of gratitude is owed to the editor, Erin-Elizabeth Johnson, for her thorough review of the initial manuscript.

All omissions and errors are the sole responsibility of the author.

Abbreviations

AER	area of enhanced risk
AFC	Asian financial crisis
ATTF	Antiterrorism Task Force (Phillipines)
CBP	Coast Guard and Border Protection
CSI	Container Security Initiative
CTF-150	Combined Task Force-150
C-TPAT	Customs-Trade Partnership Against Terrorism
DoD	Department of Defense
FoC	flag of convenience
GAO	Government Accountability Office
GFS	Global Fleet Station
GPS	Global Positioning System
IDSS	Institute of Defense and Strategic Studies
IMB	International Maritime Bureau
ISPS	International Ship and Port Facility Security
JI	*Jemaah Islamyya*
JWC	Joint War Council (Lloyd's)

KFR	kidnap for extortion
MTSA	Maritime Transport Security Act
NUMAST	National Union of Maritime Aviation and Shipping Transport Officers
PIRA	Provisional Irish Republican Army
PSI	Proliferation Security Initiative
RPG	rocket-propelled grenade
SLOC	sea-lane of communication
UNCLOS	United Nations Convention on the Law of the Sea

CHAPTER ONE

Introduction

With the collapse of the Soviet Union and the European communist eastern bloc in 1991, it was confidently assumed that the international system was on the threshold of an era of unprecedented peace and stability. Politicians, academics, and diplomats alike increasingly began to forecast the imminent establishment of a new world order that would be managed by liberal democratic institutions and would develop within the context of an integrated global economy based on the principles of the free market.[1] As this unprecedented interstate structure emerged and took root, destabilizing threats to national and international security were expected to decline commensurately.

However, the initial euphoria evoked by the end of the Cold War has been systematically replaced by a growing sense that global stability has not been achieved, and has in fact been decisively undermined by transnational security challenges, or "gray-area" phenomena. These threats, which cannot be readily defeated by the traditional defenses that states have erected to protect both their territories and populaces, reflect the remarkable fluidity that currently characterizes international politics—a setting in which it is no longer exactly apparent who can do what to whom with what means. Moreover, it has become increasingly apparent in the contemporary era that violence and the readiness

---

[1]   See, for example, The International Monetary Fund, *World Economic Outlook*, Washington, D.C., 1991, pp. 26–27.

to kill are being used by the weak to create identity, rather than simply express it.[2]

Stated more directly, the geopolitical landscape that presently confronts the global community lacks the relative stability of the linear Cold War division between East and West. Indeed, many of today's dangers are qualitatively different from classical security threats of overt military aggression stemming from a clearly defined sovereign source. Rather, security, conflict, and general threat definition have become far more opaque, diffuse, and amorphous.[3]

The maritime realm is particularly conducive to these types of threat contingencies because of its vast and largely unregulated nature. Covering 139,768,200 square miles,[4] most of this environment takes the form of high seas that lie beyond the strict jurisdiction of any one state, constituting an area that is, by definition, anarchic. These "over the horizon" oceans are fringed and linked by a complex lattice of territorial waters, estuaries, and riverine systems. These bodies of water are often poorly monitored and, according to internationally recognized jurisprudence, exist as entirely distinct and independent entities.[5] Combined, these various traits and practices have imbued the planet's aquatic expanse with the type of unpredictable and lawless qualities that Thomas Hobbes once famously wrote made life "nasty, brutish, and short."

Two specific threats that have been particularly highlighted are piracy and maritime terrorism. This monograph assesses the nature, scope, and dimensions of these two manifestations of armed violence at sea, the extent to which they are or are not interrelated, and their overall relevance to U.S. national and international security interests.

---

[2] "Terrorism and the Warfare of the Weak," *The Guardian*, October 27, 1993.

[3] Peter Chalk, *Non-Military Security and Global Order: The Impact of Extremism, Violence and Chaos on National and International Security*, London: Macmillan, 2000, pp. 1–2.

[4] This equates to approximately 2.42 times the planet's terrestrial surface area.

[5] Rupert Herbert-Burns, "Terrorism in the Early 21st Century Maritime Domain," in Joshua Ho and Catherine Zara Raymond, eds., *The Best of Times, the Worst of Times: Maritime Security in the Asia-Pacific*, Singapore: World Scientific Publishing, 2005, p. 157.

For the purposes of the analysis, the following two definitions will be used:

> *Piracy* is an act of boarding or attempting to board any ship with the apparent intent to commit theft or any other crime and with the apparent intent or capability to use force in furtherance of that act.[6]

> *Maritime terrorism* refers to the undertaking of terrorist acts and activities (1) within the maritime environment, (2) using or against vessels or fixed platforms at sea or in port, or against any one of their passengers or personnel, (3) against coastal facilities or settlements, including tourist resorts, port areas and port towns or cities.[7]

---

[6] This definition is the one used by the International Maritime Bureau (IMB). It is wider than the conceptualization adopted under the 1982 United Nations Convention on the Law of the Sea (UNCLOS), which restricts its focus only to attacks that take place on the high seas (which is problematic, because the majority of piratical incidents occur in territorial or coastal waters). The IMB definition also abolishes the traditional two-ship requirement, meaning that attacks from a raft or even the dockside would be counted as an act of piracy. See, for instance, Derek Johnson, Erika Pladdet, and Mark Valencia, "Research on Southeast Asian Piracy," in Derek Johnson and Mark Valencia, eds., *Piracy in Southeast Asia*, Singapore: Institute of Southeast Asian Studies, 2005, pp. xi–xii. Also see Commercial Crime Services, "International Maritime Bureau—Overview," Web page, 2007.

[7] This definition is used by the Council for Security Cooperation in the Asia Pacific Working Group on Maritime Terrorism. Although relatively broad, it captures the essential qualities of the phenomenon in question. See Graham Ong, "Ships Can Be Dangerous Too: Coupling Piracy and Terrorism in Southeast Asia's Maritime Security Framework," in Johnson and Valencia (2005), pp. 61–62; Sophia Quentin, "Shipping Activities: Targets of Maritime Terrorism," *MIRMAL*, Vol. 2, January 20, 2003; and Metaparti Prakash, "Maritime Terrorism: Threats to Port and Container Security and Scope for Regional Co-operation," paper presented at the 12th Meeting of the Council for Security Cooperation in the Asia Pacific Working Group on Maritime Co-operation, Singapore, December 10–11, 2002, p. 1.

CHAPTER TWO

Piracy

Scope and Dimensions

Three main types of piracy currently occur in global waters. At the low end are anchorage attacks mounted against ships at harbor. This form of piracy has exploited the relatively relaxed security procedures employed at many ports around the world. The IMB describes these types of assault as low-level armed robbery: opportunist attacks mounted close to land by small, high-speed craft crewed by maritime "muggers" normally armed with knives. Their purpose is typically to seize cash and portable high-value personal items with an average haul of $5,000–15,000.[1]

A more serious manifestation of piracy is the ransacking and robbery of vessels on the high seas or in territorial waters. This style of attack, if carried out in narrow sea-lanes, has the potential to seriously disrupt maritime navigation (especially in instances where vessels run amok because the crew is kidnapped, detained, or thrown overboard). The IMB describes these assaults as medium-level armed robbery: violent thefts involving serious injury or murder by well-organized gangs

---

[1]   Chalk, 2000, p. 58; Edward Fursdon, "Sea Piracy—or Maritime Mugging?" *INTERSEC*, Vol. 6, No. 5, May 1996, p. 166; Stanley Weeks, "Law and Order at Sea: Pacific Cooperation in Dealing with Piracy, Drugs and Illegal Migration," in Sam Bateman and Stephen Bates, eds., *Calming the Waters: Initiatives for Asia-Pacific Maritime Cooperation*, Canberra: Strategic and Defence Studies Centre, 1996, p. 44.

who usually operate from a "mother ship" and are equipped with modern weaponry.[2]

At the high end of the spectrum are assaults involving the outright theft of ships and their subsequent conversion for the purposes of illegal trading (although ship owners are also known to have arranged such attacks in order to defraud hull insurers). Often referred to as the "phantom ship" phenomenon, this form of piracy follows a typical pattern. A vessel is first seized and its cargo offloaded into lighters at sea. The ships are then renamed and reregistered under flags of convenience (FoCs)[3] and issued with false documentation to enable them to take on fresh payloads. The new cargo, which is never delivered to its intended destination, is taken to a designated port where it is sold to a buyer who is often a willing participant in the venture. The IMB describes these assaults as major criminal hijacks that are well-resourced and meticulously planned, employing highly trained and heavily armed syndicates working in conjunction with land-based operatives and brokers.[4]

A total of 2,463 actual or attempted acts of piracy were registered around the world between 2000 and the end of 2006.[5] This represents an annual average incident rate of 352, a substantial increase over the mean of 209 recorded for the period of 1994–1999 (see

---

[2]   Chalk, 2000, pp. 58, 123; Fursdon, 1996, p. 66; Mark Valencia, "Piracy and Terrorism in Southeast Asia: Similarities, Differences and Their Implications," in Johnson and Valencia, 2005, pp. 80–81.

[3]   Ships are generally reregistered with shipping bureaus in Panama, Liberia, the Bahamas, Malta, Cyprus, or Bermuda because their registration requirements are neither expensive nor stringent. See, for example, Catherine Meldrum, "Murky Waters: Financing Maritime Terrorism and Crime," *Jane's Intelligence Review*, June 2007, pp. 36–39.

[4]   Chalk, 2000, pp. 58, 62. For a good overview of the mechanics of the phantom ship phenomenon, see Jayant Abyankar, "Phantom Ships," in Eric Ellen, ed., *Shipping at Risk*, London: International Chamber of Commerce, 1997, pp. 58–75.

[5]   International Maritime Bureau, *Piracy and Armed Robbery Against Ships: Annual Report 2006*, London, 2007, p. 3; International Maritime Bureau, *Piracy and Armed Robbery Against Ships: Annual Report 2005*, London, 2006, p. 4. It should be noted that this global figure masks significant regional variations in the annual incident rate of piracy during this period. While some parts of the world were severely affected (for example, Southeast Asia and the seas off the Horn of Africa), others remained largely free of attacks (for example, North America and Western Europe).

Figure 2.1).[6] The actual problem of piracy in global waters is undoubtedly far greater than these figures suggest, since a number of attacks—possibly as many as 50 percent—are not reported. Officials with the IMB in Kuala Lumpur assert that most ship owners are reluctant to alert authorities about attacks on their vessels, largely because subsequent investigations and delays result in costs that the ship companies themselves must bear.[7] Exacerbating this reluctance is the fear that reporting incidents will merely raise maritime insurance premiums by forcing owner-operators to acknowledge that they were not practicing basic security measures (such as maintaining a regular antipiracy watch).[8] The combined magnitude of losses associated with reporting incidents would, in most cases, greatly outweigh those resulting from a piracy attack; in instances of low-level theft, ransacking, and hostage-taking, for example, costs tend to represent only two to ten percent of the value of the targeted boat and its cargo.[9]

While the overall lethality of piracy has dropped in recent years, violence continues to be a principal characteristic of many assaults. In the 515 attacks between 2005 and 2006, for instance, the IMB documented a total of 826 serious transgressions against ship crews and passengers, including 628 hostage takings, 90 kidnappings for ransom (KFR), and 54 deaths and injuries (see Table 2.1). The 440 hostage-takings in 2005 remains the highest annual figure on record.[10]

The concentration of pirate attacks continues to be greatest in Southeast Asia, especially the waters around the Indonesian archi-

---

[6] International Maritime Bureau, 2006, p. 4.

[7] According to analysts in Malaysia, the losses incurred by delays to onward journeys (known as demurrage costs) hurt ship owners the most. These losses, which can reach $20,000–30,000 per day, are especially severe in countries where police authorities lack efficiency or professionalism, both of which can result in investigations that take weeks or even months to complete. Author interviews with maritime analysts and IMB officials, Kuala Lumpur, August 26, 2006.

[8] While maintaining a vigilant antipiracy watch is probably one of the best ways to preempt a pirate attack, many ship owners do not do this because it entails hiring extra crew (which would elevate overall operating costs and therefore reduce profits).

[9] Author interviews with IMB staff and maritime analysts, Kuala Lumpur, August, 2006.

[10] International Maritime Bureau, 2007, p. 9.

Figure 2.1
Actual and Attempted Acts of Piracy, 1994–2006

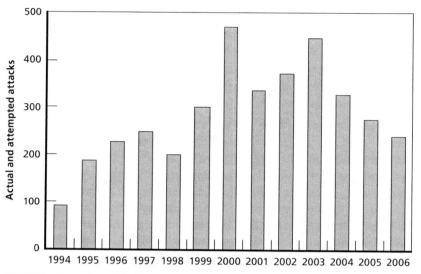

SOURCE: International Maritime Bureau, 2007.
RAND *MG697-2.1*

pelago (including stretches of the Malacca Straits that fall under the territorial jurisdiction of the Jakarta government), where roughly 21 percent of all global incidents during 2006 occurred. Other high-risk zones included the coasts and territorial seas around Nigeria, Somalia, the Gulf of Aden/Red Sea, Tanzania, Peru, Bangladesh, and Malaysia, which, collectively, accounted for half of the year's attacks (see Figure 2.2).[11] The high incidence of piracy in these areas reflects a range of factors, including growing volumes of trade, insufficient coastal/port surveillance, corruption, a lack of adequate marine policing resources, and ready access to weaponry.[12] Because these variables are directly relevant to the general surge in piracy over the last fifteen years, they are discussed in more detail below.

---

[11] International Maritime Bureau, 2007, p. 5.

[12] Author interviews with IMB staff, Kuala Lumpur, August 2006.

Table 2.1
Types of Violence to Crew and Passengers, 1995–2006

Type	1995	1996	1997	1998	1999	2000	2001	2002	2003	2004	2005	2006
Taken hostage	320	193	419	244	402	202	210	191	359	148	440	188
KFR	0	0	0	0	0	0	0	0	0	86	13	77
Threatened	59	56	119	68	21	72	45	55	65	34	14	17
Assaulted	2	9	23	58	22	9	16	9	40	12	6	2
Injured	3	9	31	37	24	99	39	38	88	59	24	15
Killed	26	26	51	78	3	72	21	10	21	32	0	15
Missing	0	0	0	0	1	26	0	24	71	30	12	3
Total for year	410	293	643	485	473	480	331	327	644	401	509	317

SOURCE: International Maritime Bureau, 2007.

Figure 2.2
Pirate Incident Locations, 2006

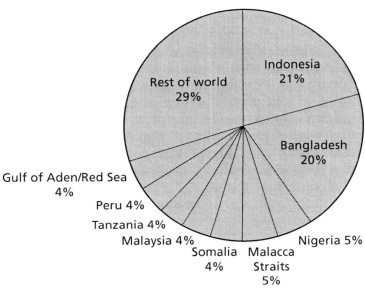

SOURCE: International Maritime Bureau, 2007.
RAND *MG697-2.2*

Factors Accounting for the Emergence of Piracy in the Contemporary Era

Seven main factors have contributed to the emergence of piracy in the contemporary era. First has been the massive increase in commercial maritime traffic. Today, roughly 80 percent of all global freight is transshipped by sea; 12 million to 15 million containers are estimated to be on the world's oceans at any one time. In 2002, this included 5.9 billion metric tons of oil and bulk commodities as well as general cargo packed in containers.[13] Combined with the large number of ports around the world—there are some 6,591 terminals currently in

---

[13] Michael Richardson, *A Time Bomb for Global Trade*, Singapore: Institute of Southeast Asian Studies, 2004, p. 3. See also Organisation for Economic Co-operation and Development, *Security in Maritime Transport: Risk Factors and Economic Impact*, Paris, July 2003, p. 3.

operation—this has provided pirates with an almost limitless range of tempting, high-payoff targets.[14]

Second is the heavy use by seaborne commercial traffic of narrow and congested maritime chokepoints near areas of endemic maritime criminal or nonstate activity, such as the Malacca Straits, the Strait of Bab el-Mandab, the Hormuz Straits, the Suez Canal, and the Panama Canal. All of these bottlenecks require ships to significantly reduce speed to ensure safe passage (in the Bosphorus Straits, for instance, at least six accidents occur every 1 million transit miles), which dramatically heightens their exposure to mid-sea interception and attack. Exacerbating this vulnerability has been the growing tendency of many shipping companies to replace full staffing complements with skeleton crews—sometimes numbering no more than a half dozen personnel—as a cost-cutting device. Although this has helped lower operating costs, it has also made hijacking much easier.[15]

Third, and specifically relevant to Southeast Asia, has been the lingering effects of the Asian financial crisis (AFC) that first broke with the forced devaluation of the Thai baht in mid-1997. This unprecedented event exerted a stronger "pull factor" on piracy, drawing more people (including members of national security forces) into maritime and other crime due to falling wages, higher food prices, and job losses. It also deprived many littoral states of the revenue required to fund effective monitoring over their coastlines.[16] These effects were particularly evident in Indonesia, an enormous archipelagic state that suffered acutely from the aftermath of the AFC. Indeed, since 1997, this coun-

---

[14] Herbert-Burns, 2005, p. 157; Joshua Sinai, "Future Trends in Worldwide Maritime Terrorism," *Connections: The Quarterly Journal*, Vol. 3, No. 1, March 2004, p. 49; and "Maritime Security Measures to Amplify Cost for Shipping," *Transport Security World*, July 29, 2003.

[15] Author interviews with government officials, intelligence analysts, and maritime security experts, Singapore, London, and Amsterdam, September 2005. See also Ali Koknar, "Maritime Terrorism: A New Challenge for NATO," *Energy Security*, January 24, 2005.

[16] Chalk, 2000, p. 61.

try's territorial waters have consistently ranked as the most pirate-prone in the world.[17]

Fourth, the general difficulties associated with maritime surveillance have been significantly heightened as a result of the events of September 11, 2001 and the concomitant pressure that has been exerted on many governments to invest in expensive land-based homeland security systems. In the case of governments that have consistently struggled to secure their sovereign waters (e.g., the Philippines, Indonesia, Turkey, Eritrea, and Kenya), these external demands have negatively affected already limited resources designated for underwriting offshore monitoring systems.[18] Policy analysts contend that the resultant void has been of particular benefit to pirate syndicates, providing them with an operational environment that is now highly conducive to their tactical and material designs.[19]

Fifth, lax coastal and port-side security have played an important role in enabling low-level piratical activity, especially harbor thefts of goods from ships at anchor. This problem has been especially acute at terminals in Nigeria, off the Horn of Africa, and across South and Southeast Asia. In many cases, there is either no functioning maritime police presence at all, or the units that are in place lack adequate staff, boats, equipment, and training. The IMB remains particularly concerned about the level of lawlessness in Somali waters (which currently rank as the most dangerous part of the world in terms of pirate violence) to the extent that it has declared all stretches within 50 miles

---

[17] Indonesia controls roughly three million square kilometers of archipelagic waters and territorial seas, plus an additional three million square kilometers of continental shelf. It has been estimated that Jakarta would require more than 300 vessels to effectively protect and monitor this expansive maritime space (as well as human resources and technology dedicated to that purpose). However, the country has only 115 vessels at its disposal, of which only 25 are fit for operating at sea at any one time. Author interviews with IMB staff, Kuala Lumpur, August 2006. See also Hasjim Djalal, "Combating Piracy: Co-operation, Needs, Efforts and Challenges," in Johnson and Valencia, 2005, p. 145.

[18] Author interviews with intelligence officials and maritime security analysts, Singapore and London, September 2005.

[19] Author interviews with maritime analysts, intelligence officials. and security experts, Washington, D.C., Singapore, London, and Amsterdam, August–September 2005.

of the shore as an effective no-go area for maritime traffic.[20] The lack of concerted port security in Bangladesh has also caused considerable consternation, prompting several major international shipping organizations to take up the issue directly with government authorities on a number of occasions.[21] Although the country has pledged to rectify the situation, a significant reduction in attacks has yet to occur. In 2003, for instance, Bangladesh recorded its highest annual piracy figures (58 incidents) since 1992. Although numbers for 2004 dropped to 17, 2005 saw a 25 percent increase by the year's end.[22]

Sixth, corruption and dysfunctional systems of national criminal justice have encouraged official complicity in high-level pirate rings, which has directly affected the phantom ship phenomenon. According to the IMB, in the Philippines, Indonesia, China and Thailand—all states where syndicates enjoy direct or at least partial access to co-opted or bribed members of the administration and bureaucracy—ships can be hijacked "to order" for approximately $300,000.[23] These insiders not only provide invaluable information about activities taking place in the maritime commercial market, they also ensure that gangs are kept abreast of actions that industry or law enforcement are taking to counter their activities.

Finally, the global proliferation of small arms has provided pirates (as well as terrorists and other criminal elements) with enhanced means to operate on a more destructive and sophisticated level.[24] The vari-

---

[20] Author interviews with IMB staff, Kuala Lumpur, August 2006. See also International Maritime Bureau, *Piracy and Armed Robbery Against Ships: Report for the Period 1 January—30 September 2005*, London, November 8, 2005, p. 23.

[21] International Maritime Bureau, *Piracy and Armed Robbery Against Ships: Report for the Period 1 January–30 June 2006*, p. 20; Chalk, 2000, p. 74. Similar concerns about the security at Bangladeshi ports were expressed to the author during interviews with security analysts in Bangkok, September 2006.

[22] International Maritime Bureau, 2006, p. 5.

[23] See Abyankar, 1997, pp. 69–70.

[24] Overviews of the dynamics of the contemporary light arms trade can be found in Aaron Karp, "Small Arms—The New Major Weapons," in Jeffrey Boutwell and Michael T. Klare, eds., *Lethal Commerce: The Global Trade in Small Arms and Light Weapons*, Cambridge, Mass.: American Academy of Sciences, 1995; Michael T. Klare, "An Avalanche of Guns:

ety of weaponry currently available on global black markets is truly enormous. Originating from sources in Africa, Asia, and Europe, it includes anything from pistols, light/heavy machine guns, and automatic assault rifles to antiship mines, handheld mortars, and rocket-propelled grenades (RPGs).[25] Most commentators agree that ready access to these munitions—most of which are readily transportable, easy to handle, cheap, and durable—is one of the main factors contributing to the growing level of violence that has come to typify piracy in recent years. As the current director of the IMB's office in Kuala Lumpur, Noel Choong, remarks: "Five to six years ago, when pirates attacked, they used machetes, knives, and pistols. Today, they come equipped with AK-47s, M-16s, rifle grenades, and RPGs."[26]

The Dangers of Piracy

The dangers associated with contemporary piracy are complex and multifaceted, having direct implications for human, political, economic, and environmental security. At the most basic level, attacks constitute a direct threat to the lives and welfare of the citizens of a variety of flag states. As noted above, strikes are frequently violent and can be expected to involve casualties. Disturbingly, there has been a marked rise in physical assaults, with the 440 hostage takings in 2005

Light Weapons Trafficking and Armed Conflict in the Post-Cold War Era," in Mary Kaldor and Basker Vashee, eds., *New Wars: Restructuring the Global Military Sector*, London: Pinter, 1997; Andrew Latham, "The Light Weapons Problem: Causes, Consequences and Policy Options," in Andrew Latham, ed., *Multilateral Approaches to Non-Proliferation: Proceedings of the 4th Canadian Non-Proliferation Workshop*, Toronto: Centre for International and Security Studies, 1996; Anthony Davis, "Tracing the Dynamics of the Illicit Arms Trade," *Jane's Intelligence Review*, September 2003; Paul Eavis, "Awash with Light Weapons," *The World Today*, April 1999; Chris Smith, "Light Weapons Proliferation: A Global Survey," *Jane's Intelligence Review*, July 1999; and Klare, "The Kalashnikov Age," *Bulletin of the Atomic Scientists*, Vol. 55, No. 1, January/February 1999.

[25] Chalk, 2000, pp. 65–66.

[26] Author interviews with IMB staff, Kuala Lumpur, August 2006. See also P. Mukundan, "The Scourge of Piracy in Southeast Asia: Can Any Improvements be Expected in the Near Future?" in Johnson and Valencia, 2005, p. 39.

remaining the highest figure on record. Although the overall number of these incidents dropped in 2006, they were still significant at a total of 188.[27] As one senior member of the United Kingdom's National Union of Maritime, Aviation and Shipping Transport Officers (NUMAST) remarks: "The necessities of normal diplomacy should not obscure the fact that British nationals are being threatened with extreme violence. The present intolerable situation should be approached by the UK government just as firmly as if British tourists were being attacked whilst [taking a holiday] in a [foreign] country."[28]

Quite apart from the risk of death and physical injury, many seafarers who have been subjected to a pirate attack have suffered considerable mental trauma. Many of those who do not fully recover never go to sea again. Despite this, the human cost involved in modern-day piracy is seldom recognized, largely because assaults tend to be directed against "less than visible" targets. Again, NUMAST remarks: "If you had civilian aircraft being threatened or bazookas being fired at train drivers, there would be a public outcry. Because it is shipping, it's out of sight, out of mind, and nothing is done."[29]

Piracy also has a direct economic impact in terms of fraud, stolen cargos, delayed trips, and higher insurance premiums. In addition, it could potentially undermine a maritime state's trading ability.[30] As previously noted, ship owners are often required to pay their own legal expenses for postattack investigations, and they always have to bear the costs of cancelled or interrupted onward journeys. The costs of major criminal hijackings can be particularly exorbitant; on a number of occasions, consignees have had to shoulder the entire loss from phan-

---

[27] International Maritime Bureau, 2007, p. 9.

[28] *NUMAST Telegraph*, Vol. 25, No. 7, Piracy Supplement, July 1992, p. i.

[29] Captain Graeme Hicks, secretary of NUMAST, as cited in "For Those in Peril on the Sea," *The Economist*, August 9, 1997.

[30] It should be noted that no systematic study of the overall cost of piracy has ever been undertaken, particularly in relation to expenses incurred as a result of suppression. Moreover, the impunity of many attacks makes accurate records of losses difficult to gather, while analysts only infrequently disclose the contents of any given calculation. See Martin Murphy, *Contemporary Piracy and Maritime Terrorism: The Threat to International Security*, London: International Institute for Strategic Studies, Adelphi Paper 338, 2007, p. 19.

tom ship frauds.[31] Moreover, a reputation for piracy has the potential to damage the international standing of a trading country and could lead to a boycott of its port facilities. This became a major concern for Hong Kong in the mid-1990s, when many shipping companies threatened to boycott the territory's port facilities as a result of the frequency of attacks in what had become known as the Hainan–Luzon–Hong Kong terror triangle.[32] More recently, similar problems have beset terminals in Bangladesh, Nigeria, Indonesia, and the Horn of Africa.[33] Overall, the IMB estimates that piracy costs the shipping industry anywhere from $1 billion to $16 billion a year.[34] Although this figure might appear unacceptable, it is generally viewed as an inevitable cost of doing business that, when measured against the annual value of maritime commerce—which in 2005 totalled $7.8 trillion[35]—is not, in fact, prohibitively onerous.

Politically, piracy can play a pivotal role in undermining and weakening regime legitimacy by encouraging corruption among elected government officials. This has been a recurrent problem in Indonesia, where numerous shipping associations and maritime bodies decry the complicity of government officials and members of the security forces

---

[31] One noteworthy case concerned the 1995 seizure of the *Anna Sierra*, which, when eventually discovered at the port of Bei Hei, was registered under the name *Arctic Sea*. By the time the vessel was released, losses from cargo theft, the imposition of a "finder's fee" by Chinese authorities, and post-incident investigations had run into the millions of U.S. dollars. All costs were ultimately borne by the ship's rightful owners. See International Maritime Bureau, *Piracy and Armed Robbery Against Ships: Special Report*, London: International Chamber of Commerce, 1997, pp. 33–39.

[32] See, for instance, Robert Beckman, Carl Grundy-Warr, and Vivian Forbes, "Acts of Piracy in the Malacca Straits," *Maritime Briefing*, Vol. 1, No. 4, 1994; Kazuo Takita and Bob Couttie, "ASEAN Pressured to Act Against Pirates," *Lloyds List*, May 29, 1992, p. 3; and Michael Pugh, "Piracy and Armed Robbery at Sea: Problems and Remedies," *Low Intensity Conflict and Law Enforcement*, Vol. 2, No. 1, 1993, p. 11.

[33] Author interviews with IMB staff, Kuala Lumpur, August 2006.

[34] See, for example, Joshua Ho, "Security of Sea-Lanes in Southeast Asia," unpublished paper, Indian Observer Research Foundation, Workshop on Maritime Counterterrorism, New Delhi, November 29–30, 2004.

[35] Murphy, 2007, p. 21; World Trade Organization, *International Trade Statistics 2006*, Table 1.3, November 2006, p. 15.

who participate in, arrange, or otherwise facilitate both low- and high-end attacks.[36] Although Jakarta has pledged to crack down on manifestations of state complicity in piracy, it lacks the resources to do so on a comprehensive basis.

Attacks also have the potential to trigger a major environmental disaster, particularly if they take place in crowded sea-lanes traversed by heavily laden oil tankers. The nightmare scenario is a major crash taking place between an unmanned rogue vessel and an oil tanker. The resulting discharge of petroleum would cause irreparable damage to maritime life and other offshore resources. If left to drift, the slick could also seriously degrade large tracts of fertile coastal lowland, which could seriously affect any state that relies on the ocean as a primary source of protein for domestic consumption or regional export.[37] In the opinion of the IMB, it is only a matter of time before pirates trigger an environmental disaster of this sort.[38]

---

[36] Author interviews with IMB staff and maritime analysts, Kuala Lumpur, August 2006.

[37] See, for example, Greg Chaikin, "Piracy in Asia: International Co-operation and Japan's Role," in Johnson and Valencia (2005), p. 127; and Abyankar, "Piracy and Ship Robbery: A Growing Menace," in Hamzah Ahmad and Akira Ogawa, eds., *Combating Piracy and Ship Robbery*, Tokyo: Okazaki Institute, 2001.

[38] Valencia, "Piracy and Politics in Southeast Asia," in Johnson and Valencia, 2005, p. 114.

CHAPTER THREE

Maritime Terrorism

Historically, the world's oceans have not been a major locus of terrorist activity. Indeed, according to the RAND Terrorism Database, strikes on maritime targets and assets have constituted only two percent of all international incidents over the last 30 years. To be sure, part of the reason for this relative paucity has to do with the fact that many terrorist organizations have neither been located near coastal regions nor possessed the means to extend their physical reach beyond purely local theaters. There are also several problems associated with carrying out waterborne strikes which have, at least historically, helped to offset some of the tactical advantages associated with esoteric maritime environments outlined in Chapter Two. Most intrinsically, operating at sea requires terrorists to have mariner skills, access to appropriate assault and transport vehicles, the ability to mount and sustain operations from a non-land–based environment, and certain specialist capabilities (for example, surface and underwater demolition techniques).[1] Limited resources have traditionally prevented groups from accessing these options.

Very much related to this is the fact that terrorists are inherently conservative when it comes to choosing attack modalities. Precisely because they are constrained by ceilings in operational finance and

---

[1] Author interviews with Institute of Defense and Strategic Studies (IDSS) staff, Singapore, September 2005. See also Paul Wilkinson, "Terrorism and the Maritime Environment" and Brian Jenkins, Bonnie Cordes, Karen Gardela, and Geraldine Petty, "A Chronology of Terrorist Attacks and Other Criminal Actions Against Maritime Targets," both in Eric Ellen, ed., *Violence at Sea*, Paris: International Chamber of Commerce, 1986.

skill sets, most groups have chosen to follow the path of least resistance. They adhere to the tried and tested methods that are known to work, that offer reasonably high chances of success, and whose consequences can be relatively easily predicted. Stated more directly, in a world of finite human and material assets, the costs and unpredictability associated with expanding to the maritime realm have typically trumped any potential benefits that might be garnered from initiating such a change in operational direction.

A further consideration has to do with the nature of maritime targets themselves: Because they are out of sight, they are generally out of mind (this is particularly true of commercial vessels). Thus, an attack on a ship is less likely to elicit the same publicity—either in scope or immediacy—as a strike on land-based targets, which, because they are fixed and typically located near urban areas, are far more media-accessible (although, as argued below, this point may not apply with respect to contingencies involving heavily-laden cruise liners and ferries).[2] This consideration is important because terrorism, at root, is a tactic that can only be effective if it is able to *visibly* demonstrate its salience and relevance through the propaganda of the deed.[3] Rather like the philosopher's tree silently falling in the forest, if no one observes the event, does it have any reason for being?

In spite of these considerations, there has been a modest yet highly discernible spike in high-profile terrorist incidents at sea over the past six years, the more notable of which are described in the appendix to this monograph. In addition, there has been a spate of significant maritime terrorist plots that have been preempted before execution. These planned strikes, most of which have been directly connected to al Qaeda and its affiliates,[4] included an aborted attack against the USS

---

[2]   Wilkinson, 1986, p. 34; Jenkins et al., 1986, p. 65.

[3]   For a discussion on this aspect of the terrorist phenomenon, see Peter Chalk, *West European Terrorism and Counter-Terrorism: The Evolving Dynamic*, London: Macmillan, 1996, Chapter One.

[4]   Most of al Qaeda's planned maritime attacks were the brainchild of Abdel Rahim al-Nashiri (colloquially known as Ameer al Bahr, or "Prince of the Seas"). Arrested in 2003, he admitted to being the mastermind behind the bombings of the USS *Cole* and M/V *Limburg* as well as the chief architect of al Qaeda's maritime terror agenda. His strategy involved four

The Sullivans in January 2000,[5] additional bombings of U.S. naval ships sailing in Singaporean, Malaysian, and Indonesian waters, suicide strikes against Western shipping interests in the Mediterranean, small boat rammings of supertankers transiting the Straits of Gibraltar, and attacks on cruise liners carrying Israeli tourists to Turkey.[6]

Combined, these various incidents have galvanized fears in the West that terrorists, especially militants connected with the international jihadist network, are moving to decisively extend operational mandates beyond purely land-based theaters. These concerns have been particularly evident in the United States, which has been at the forefront of attempts to strengthen the global maritime security regime in the post-9/11 era.

Five main factors seem salient in rationalizing the presumed shift in extremist focus to water-based environments. First, many of the vulnerabilities that have encouraged a higher rate of pirate attacks also apply to terrorism, including inadequate coastal surveillance, lax port security, a profusion of targets, the overwhelming dependence of maritime trade on passage through congested chokepoints (where vessels are exposed to attacks), and an increased tendency to staff vessels with skeleton crews. Because these gaps and weaknesses persist at a time when littoral states are devoting more resources to land-based

---

main components: ramming ships with explosive-laden Zodiacs as a ramming device (i.e., the same sort of attack that was used against the *Cole* and *Limburg*); detonating medium-sized vessels and trawlers near warships, cruise liners, or ports; crashing planes into large carriers such as supertankers; and employing suicide divers or underwater demolition teams to destroy surface platforms. See Eric Watkins, "Security—Al'Qa'eda Suspect Admits Role in Limburg," *Lloyd's List*, January 21, 2003; Valencia, 2005a, p. 83; and "Al Qaeda Has Multi-Faceted Marine Strategy," Agence France Press, January 20, 2003.

5   The aborted strike on *The Sullivans* was carried out as part of the 2000 millennium terrorist plots. The plan called for the detonation of a small suicide boat as it pulled alongside the U.S. vessel. The attack craft was so overloaded with explosives, however, that it sank, causing the operation to be called off.

6   Bronson Percival, *Indonesia and the United States: Shared Interests in Maritime Security*, Washington, D.C.: United States-Indonesia Society, June 2005, p. 9; Richardson, 2004, p. 19; Ong, 2005, p. 51; Murad Sezer, "Turkish Court Charges Suspected al-Qaeda Militant," Associated Press, August 10, 2005; and "Security Fears Keep Israeli Ships from Turkey," *The New York Times*, August 9, 2005.

security structures (as discussed above), they are amplifying—in relative terms—the attractive qualities of what is already a highly opaque operational setting. In other words, these gaps and weaknesses provide extremists with an opportunity to move, hide, and strike in a manner that is not possible in a terrestrial theater.[7]

Second, the growth of commercial enterprises specializing in maritime sports and equipment has arguably provided terrorists with a readily accessible conduit through which to avail themselves of the necessary training and resources for operating at sea.[8] In the southern Philippines, for example, members of the Indonesian-based *Jemaah Islamyya* (JI) network are known to have enrolled in scuba courses run by commercial or resort diving companies. Members of the local security forces widely believe that the main purpose for taking these lessons has been to facilitate underwater attacks against gas and oil pipelines off the coast of Mindanao.[9]

Third, maritime attacks offer terrorists an additional means of causing economic destabilization. One common scenario expressed by analysts and government officials is an attack designed to shut down a port or block a critical sea-lane of communication (SLOC) in order to disrupt the mechanics of the "just in time, just enough" global maritime trade complex.[10] Indicative of this line of thinking is the following commentary made by Michael Richardson, a senior analyst with the Institute of Southeast Asian Studies in Singapore:

> The global economy is built on integrated supply chains that feed components and other materials to users just before they

---

[7] Author interviews with maritime analysts and intelligence officials, Washington, D.C., Singapore, London, and Amsterdam, August–September 2005.

[8] See, for instance, Jenkins et al., 1986, p. 67.

[9] Author interviews with intelligence and law enforcement personnel, Manila, May 2005 and Singapore, September 2005. What appears to have particularly attracted the attention of regional authorities is that the alleged JI members actively sought training in deep-sea water diving but exhibited little or no interest in decompression techniques.

[10] Author interviews with Control Risks Group and Lloyd's, London and Amsterdam, September 2005. See also Catherine Zara Raymond, "Maritime Terrorism, A Risk Assessment: The Australian Example," in Ho and Raymond, 2005, p. 179.

are required and just in the right amounts. That way, inventory costs are kept low. [However, because these supply chains have no excess capacity,] if they are disrupted, it will have repercussions around the world, profoundly affecting business confidence.[11]

Although it is true that very little redundancy (in the form of surplus supply) is built into the contemporary international trading system, it would be extremely difficult to decisively disrupt its operation through a campaign of terrorism. Major ports such as Rotterdam, Vancouver, Singapore, New York, and Los Angeles are both expansive and highly secure, making them extremely difficult to fully close down. Even if an attack did result in the wholesale suspension of all loading/offloading functions, ships could be fairly easily diverted (albeit at a cost) to alternative terminals, thus ensuring the continued integrity of the inter-modal transportation network. Successfully blocking a SLOC to all through traffic would be similarly difficult, not least because it would require a group to scuttle several large vessels at the same time—a formidable and technically demanding undertaking.[12] Moreover, very few maritime choke points are truly nonsubstitutable for ocean-bound freight. Bypassing the Malacca Straits in Southeast Asia (one of the world's busiest maritime corridors), for instance, would require only an extra three days of steaming, and other than oil and certain perishable goods, most commodities would not be unduly affected by short delays in delivery.[13]

While long-term or widespread disruption to the global economy is unlikely, it is certainly possible that temporary, localized fiscal damage could result from an act of terrorism. The suicide strike on the M/V *Limburg* in 2002 is a case in point. Although the incident only

---

[11] Richardson, 2004, p. 7.

[12] Sinking any sizeable vessel with a high waterline would require the perpetrating group to have access to a large quantity of explosives, the time and means to transport this material, and the expertise to know where to place bombs to cause a critical hull breach. Overcoming these logistical and knowledge barriers would be very difficult for a single attack, much less an assault that targeted two or three ships.

[13] Author interviews with maritime experts and intelligence analysts, Singapore, London, and Amsterdam, September 2005.

resulted in three deaths (including the two bombers), it directly contributed to a short-term collapse of international shipping business in the Gulf, led to a 48 cent per barrel hike in the price of Brent crude oil, and due to the tripling of war risks premiums levied on ships calling at Aden, resulted in a 93-percent drop in container terminal throughput that cost the Yemeni economy an estimated $3.8 million a month in port revenues.[14]

It is also worth bearing in mind that maritime terrorism, to the extent that it does have at least a residual disruptive economic potential, resonates with the underlying operational and ideological rationale of al Qaeda and the wider global jihadist "nebula." Indeed, attacking key pillars of the Western commercial, trading, and energy system is a theme that, at least rhetorically, has become increasingly prominent in the years since 9/11, and that is viewed as integral to the Islamist war on the United States and its major allies. Portraying the attacks on the World Trade Center and Pentagon as a single defining point in exposing the fallacy of American (financial) power,[15] Bin Laden and his chief "lieutenant," Ayman al-Zawahiri, have both squarely put the thrust of their continuing campaign against Washington in the context of economic war.[16] This was made explicitly apparent in a video

---

[14] See Ben Sheppard, "Maritime Security Measures," *Jane's Intelligence Review*, March 2003, p. 55; Richardson, 2004, p. 70; Herbert-Burns, 2005, p. 165; Valencia, 2005b, p. 84; and Vivian Ho, "No Let Down in Global Pirate Attacks by Pirates," Kyodo News Service, July 24, 2003.

[15] For more on the financial fallout of the 9/11 attacks, see Lloyd Dixon and Robert T. Reville, "National Security and Compensation Policy for Terrorism Losses," in *Catastrophic Risks and Insurance: Policy Issues in Insurance*, Paris: Organization for Economic Co-operation and Development, 2006; Lloyd Dixon and Rachel Kaganoff Stern, *Compensation for Losses from the 9/11 Attacks*, Santa Monica, Calif.: RAND Corporation, MG-264-ICJ, 2004; and Peter Chalk, Bruce Hoffman, Robert T. Reville, and Anna-Britt Kasupski, *Trends in Terrorism: Threats to the United States and the Future of the Terrorism Risk Insurance Act*, Santa Monica, Calif.: RAND Corporation, MG-393-CTRMP, 2005.

[16] In 2004, Bin Laden specifically referred to a "bleed to bankruptcy strategy" aimed at inflicting an unsustainable cost burden on the United States and its allies. It is unclear whether the intent to cause economic disruption is more rhetorical than substantive in nature. For additional details concerning al Qaeda's presumed emphasis on (asymmetric) economic targeting, see Matthew Hunt, "Bleed to Bankruptcy," *Jane's Intelligence Review*, January 2007, pp. 14–17.

statement released by the al Qaeda emir in December 2004, when he reflected on a guerrilla conflict in Afghanistan that had "bled Russia for ten years until it went bankrupt," affirming that al Qaeda is "continuing in the same policy to make the US bleed profusely to the point of bankruptcy."[17]

Fourth, sea-based terrorism constitutes a viable means of inflicting "mass coercive punishment" on enemy audiences. Cruise ships and passenger ferries are especially relevant in this regard, largely because they cater to large numbers of people who are confined in a single physical space[18] (which, like aircraft, makes them ideal venues for carrying out assaults aimed at maximizing civilian casualties), sail according to set and publicly available schedules (which provides transparency in preattack planning), are characterized by variable standards of dock-side security (something that is particularly true of ferries),[19] remain vulnerable to post-departure interception (at least compared to civil aviation), and, in the case of passenger ferries, have certain design features that make them susceptible to cataclysmic assault (vehicle ferries, for instance, are notoriously easy to capsize because they lack stabilizing bulkheads on their lower car/truck decks).[20] Moreover, because

---

[17] Bin Laden, as cited in Hunt, 2007, p. 16; Douglas Jehl and David Johnston, "In Video Message, bin Laden Issues Warning to U.S." *New York Times*, October 30, 2004.

[18] This is especially true of ferries in the developing world, which often operate at full or more than full capacity.

[19] While the absence of dock-side security is most acute in resource-depleted developing littoral states, questions have also been raised with respect to advanced maritime states. In the United States, for instance, relative spending on port security has been criticized as wholly insufficient to contemporary needs. Various audits carried out at the federal level have shown that while Washington has invested upwards of $18 billion in safeguarding the nation's airports from terrorist attack, only $630 million has been allocated for augmenting security at major maritime terminals. See Robert Block, "Security Gaps Already Plague Ports," *The Wall Street Journal*, February 23, 2006.

[20] Interviews with maritime security analysts and intelligence officials, Singapore, London, and Amsterdam, September 2005. For an in-depth discussion of the vulnerabilities of passenger shipping and their relative vulnerability to terrorist attack, see Michael Greenberg, Peter Chalk, Henry Willis, Ivan Khilko, and David Ortiz, *Maritime Terrorism: Risk and Liability*, Santa Monica, Calif.: RAND Corporation, MG-520-CTRMP 2006, Chapters Five and Six.

cruise ships cater to rich, middle-class American and European tourists, these vessels provide the type of high-prestige, iconic target that would likely resonate with extremist Islamist intent[21] and elicit considerable media attention if decisively struck.[22]

The bombing of the *SuperFerry 14* in the Philippines graphically underscores how easily mass casualties could result from a concerted attack against passenger shipping. The operation, which left more than 116 people dead, involved a total planning cycle of only a couple months, was executed with a very crude improvised explosive device—16 sticks of dynamite secreted in a hollowed-out television set—and cost no more than PS19,000 (approximately $400) to pull off. As one senior official with the Philippine Anti-Terrorism Task Force (ATTF) remarked, the incident demonstrated the acute vulnerability of ferries to sabotage—one that could realistically spark copycat strikes by groups intent on maximizing civilian damage with minimal expenditure.[23]

Finally, the expansive global container-shipping complex offers terrorists a logistical channel that favors the covert movement of weapons and personnel. Most commentators generally agree that terrorist contingencies involving this class of vessel are more likely to involve exploitation of the cargo supply chain than attacks directed against carriers themselves. Merchant craft are not only large, they also have a high waterline, which means that a considerable quantity of explosives would be needed to cause a critical breach. Even if sufficient quanti-

---

[21] The fact that cruise ships cater to a mostly American and European customer base may also mean that attacks against these vessels carry relatively little risk of negatively affecting wider Arab/Asian Islamic interests. This is not necessarily the case with land-based venues, as bombings of Western embassies in Kenya and Tanzania (1998), tourist resorts in Bali (2002 and 2005), and hotels in Jakarta and Amman (2003 and 2005 respectively)—all of which resulted in high casualty rates for local Muslims—clearly demonstrated.

[22] Indeed, as the November 2005 assault against the *Seaborne Spirit* off the Horn of Africa demonstrates, even comparatively small-scale events have the potential to elicit considerable international media attention and interest. The liner, which was en route from Egypt to Mombassa with 302 passengers and crew, was strafed with machine gun fire and RPGs while sailing 70 nautical miles off the Somali coast. Although no one was seriously hurt in the attack, the incident caught the headlines of major newspapers around the world, many of which specifically focused on the fact that the vessel was carrying mostly Western tourists.

[23] Author interview with ATTF, Manila, November 2005.

ties could be smuggled aboard hidden in a container, there would be no way of ensuring that the targeted crate would be loaded and placed in a position that could allow a bomb to be detonated with maximum effect.[24]

By contrast, leveraging container carriers for logistical purposes is not only viable, but also relatively easy. This is largely because the international trading system is deliberately designed to be as open and accessible as possible (to keep costs low and turnover high), which necessarily means minimizing the disruptive impact of any security measures thereby instituted. Reflecting this, only two to five percent of containers shipped around the world are physically inspected at their port of arrival.[25] Simply put, the statistical probability of successfully smuggling a weapon or bomb is much greater than the probability of intercepting one.[26]

Just as importantly, the highly complex nature of the containerized supply chain creates a plethora of openings for terrorist infiltration. Unlike other cargo vessels that typically handle payloads for a single customer loaded at port, container ships deal with commodities from hundreds of companies and individuals that, in most cases,

---

[24] It should also be noted that there would be little immediate impact associated with sinking a commercial carrier, either in terms of attracting mass-media attention or eliciting public concern (let alone terror) by triggering major economic externalities.

[25] John Fritelli, *Port and Maritime Security: Background and Issues for Congress*, Washington, D.C.: Congressional Research Service, December 30, 2004, p. 4; Raymond, 2005, p. 187.

[26] It should be noted that certain commentators believe that the heightened focus on containerized shipping will, by default, cause terrorists and criminals to opt for other, more secure maritime smuggling and weapon delivery methods. Options that have been highlighted include welding arms cases and/or bombs to a vessel's hull (mimicking methods that are known to have been used by drug cartels to smuggle narcotics) and trafficking weapons in craft that are unlikely to draw suspicion (such as fishing trawlers). Another scenario is the disbursement of consignments via a piggy-backed "two-ship" ejection approach, which essentially involves dispatching a weapons-laden speedboat below the waterline from the submersed stern of a tug. According to security officials, as long as the vessel carrying the munitions has been properly sealed, it would float to the surface without damage. Author interviews with security analysts, Bangkok, September 2006.

are received and transported from inland warehouses.[27] Each point of transfer along this spectrum of movement is a potential source of vulnerability for the overall integrity of the cargo and provides extremists with numerous opportunities to "stuff" or otherwise tamper with boxed crates.[28] Compounding the situation is the highly rudimentary nature of the locks that are used to seal containers, the bulk of which consist of little more than plastic ties or bolts that can be quickly cut and then reattached using a combination of superglue and heat.[29]

Underscoring all of these considerations is the ineffectiveness of point of origin inspections. Many littoral states fail to routinely vet dock workers,[30] do not require that truck drivers present valid identification before entering an offloading facility,[31] and frequently over-

---

[27] For even a standard consignment, numerous parties and agents would be involved, including the exporter, the importer, the freight forwarder, a customs broker, excise inspectors, commercial trucking/railroad firms, dock workers, possibly harbor feeder craft, and the ocean carrier itself.

[28] Fritelli, 2004, p. 9.

[29] Author interviews with Department of Homeland Security Liaison officials, Singapore and London, September 2005. See also Greenberg et al., 2006, p. 4. Most commercial shipping companies have been reluctant to develop more robust seals given the costs involved, and because even newer systems cannot offer anything approaching 100 percent infallibility. A standard (plastic) lock can be purchased for a few cents if ordered in bulk, whereas more resistant versions might cost several hundreds of dollars. Moves to develop so-called "smart boxes" equipped with GPS transponders and radio frequency identification devices that emit warning signals if they are interfered with have run into similar problems and had not, at the time of writing, been embraced with any real degree of enthusiasm by the international maritime industry.

[30] This is true of both small and large terminals. Privacy regulations in the Netherlands, for instance, preclude the option of comprehensive security vetting for dock workers without first gaining their permission. In the words of one Dutch expert: "I would be amazed if harbor employees at Rotterdam, Antwerp, or Amsterdam were required to undergo any mandatory criminal background check." Author interview with Control Risks Group, Amsterdam, September 2005.

[31] Again, these problems are not unique to the developing world. In the United States, some 11,000 truck drivers enter and leave the Long Beach terminal in Los Angeles with only a standard driver's license. Singapore, which runs arguably one of the world's most sophisticated and well-protected commercial maritime ports, does not require shipping companies to declare goods on their vessels if they are only transiting through the city-state's territorial waters (largely due to a fear that if this was made mandatory, the resulting red tape would

look the need to ensure that all cargo is accompanied by an accurate manifest. The absence of uniform and concerted dockside safeguards works to the direct advantage of the terrorist, both because it is virtually impossible to inspect containers once they are on the high seas and due to the fact that only a tiny fraction of boxed freight is actually checked on arrival at its destination.

---

deflect trade north to Malaysia). As a result, the government does not know what is being transported on most of carriers that pass through the country. Author interviews with maritime experts and government officials, Singapore, September 2005. See also Block, 2006.

CHAPTER FOUR

A Piracy–Terrorism Nexus?

Complicating the maritime threat picture is growing speculation that a tactical nexus could emerge between piracy and terrorism. One of the main concerns is that extremist groups will seek to overcome existing operational constraints in sea-based capabilities by working in conjunction with or subcontracting out missions to maritime crime gangs and syndicates. Various scenarios have been postulated, including the possible employment of pirates to seize and deliver a liquefied-natural-gas carrier that is then used as a floating bomb, scuttle a large oceangoing vessel in a narrow SLOC either to disrupt maritime trade or precipitate a major environmental disaster, or hijack a freighter and reregister it under an FoC as a phantom ship.

The presumed convergence between maritime terrorism and piracy remains highly questionable, however. To date, there has been no credible evidence to support speculation about this nexus.[1] Moreover, the objectives of the two actors remain entirely distinct. The business of piracy is directly dependent on a thriving and active global shipping industry and is aimed at profit. In contrast, terrorists—at least in the context of the contemporary jihadist network—are assumed to be seeking the destruction of the global maritime trade network as part of their self-defined economic war against the West.[2] As Young and Valencia note, piracy is predicated on financial gain while terrorism is

---

[1] Author interview with IMB, Kuala Lumpur, August 2006.

[2] Author interviews with maritime experts and intelligence officials, Singapore, London, and Amsterdam, September 2005.

motivated by political goals beyond the immediate act of attacking a maritime target; the former will eschew attention and aim to sustain their trade while the latter will court publicity and inflict as much damage as possible.[3]

The above considerations notwithstanding, the possibility of a nexus emerging between piracy and terrorism has certainly informed the perceptions of governments, international organizations, and major shipping interests around the world. There have been persistent, though unverified, reports of political extremists boarding vessels in Southeast Asia in an apparent effort to learn how to pilot them for a rerun of 9/11 at sea.[4] One such alleged case involved the seizure of the *Dewi Madrim* in 2003. Although the exact circumstances surrounding the incident remain unclear, it is known that the raiding party steered the commandeered ship for nearly an hour before escaping with some equipment and technical documents. The official position of the IMB is that the attack was a pure act of piracy and that any connection to terrorism was a product of media misrepresentation and sensationalism.[5] However, various other analysts reject this interpretation and insist that the takeover was a training exercise designed to hone the navigation and sailing skills of terrorists intent on ramming an ocean-going vessel into a very large crude carrier, a major port such as Singapore, or an offshore petrochemical facility.[6]

---

[3]   Adam Young and Mark Valencia, "Piracy and Terrorism Threats Overlap," *The Washington Times*, July 7, 2003; Young and Valencia, "Conflation of Piracy and Terrorism in Southeast Asia: Rectitude and Utility," *Contemporary Southeast Asia*, Vol. 25, No. 2, August 2003, p. 267.

[4]   Murphy, "Maritime Terrorism: Threat in Context," *Jane's Intelligence Review*, February 2006, p. 23.

[5]   Author interviews with IMB, London, September 2005.

[6]   Author interviews with IMB, Kuala Lumpur, August 2006. See also Percival, 2005, p. 10, and Rommel Banaloi, "Maritime Terrorism in Southeast Asia," *Naval War College Review*, Vol. 58, No. 4, Autumn 2005, p. 65. According to the IMB in Malaysia, the skills needed to undertake an operation of this sort are not particularly daunting, particularly since modern carriers are equipped with autopilot and navigation systems. As one official remarked: "Within two months any competent terrorist could master the fundamentals involved in seizing and steering a ship to be used as a weapon."

The specter of a pirate-terrorism nexus attracted some political controversy in 2005 when the Lloyd's Joint War Council (JWC) designated the Malacca Straits as an area of enhanced risk (AER). This determination was made by the JWC on the basis of a threat assessment conducted by the U.K.-based Aegis Group, which expressly considered anticipated links between regional Islamist militants—specifically those connected to the JI network—and maritime criminals operating from Indonesian waters.[7]

The designation was vociferously rejected by all three Malacca states, who argued that the Aegis group has no recognized presence in the region, that the assessment was not aligned with the empirical risk of attack (terrorist or pirate) in the Malacca Straits (especially in light of a comparison between the number of incidents that have occurred and the volume of traffic passing through the Straits), and that the report itself offered no solid evidence of even marginal links emerging between piracy and terrorism in the region.[8] However, Lloyd's backed the credibility of the Aegis assessment, pointing out that it was hardly surprising that Indonesia, Malaysia, and Singapore would reject the findings given the added costs that could be legitimately imposed on ships using the waterway (and thus spur commercial vessels to seek cheaper corridors).[9]

---

[7] Author interviews with Lloyd's, IDSS, Raytheon (ASEAN) International, and Glenn Defense Marine (Asia), London, and Singapore, September 2005.

[8] Author interviews with maritime experts, Singapore, September 2005.

[9] Author interviews with Lloyd's, London, September 2005. The designation of the Malacca Straits as an AER allows maritime insurance companies to levy a war surcharge on ships transiting the waterway up to 0.10 percent of the total value of their cargo; this is over and above the 0.05 percent baseline premium that is routinely imposed on seaborne freight. The Straits were removed from the Lloyd's list in mid-2006, ostensibly on the grounds that the percentage of attacks had dropped enough to warrant the reinstatement of the waterway's status as safe conduit for maritime trade. Author interviews with maritime analysts and IMB officials, Kuala Lumpur, August 2006.

CHAPTER FIVE

Relevance to the United States

As one of the globe's principal maritime trading states, accounting for nearly 20 percent (measured in metric tons) of all international sea-borne freight in any given year, the United States has a direct, vested interest in securing the world's oceanic environment. Commercial carriers transport more than 95 percent of the country's non–Northern American trade by weight and 75 percent by value. Commodities shipped by sea currently constitute a full quarter of U.S. gross domestic product, more than double the figure recorded in 1970.

Besides economic considerations, the marine transportation system plays an important role in U.S. national security. The Departments of Defense and Transportation have jointly designated 17 American ports—13 of which also act as commercial trading hubs—as strategic because they are necessary to expedite major military deployments.[1] In the view of the Government Accountability Office, if these terminals were decisively attacked, "not only could ... civilian casualties be sustained, but DoD [Department of Defense] could also lose precious cargo and time and be forced to rely heavily on its [already] overburdened airlift capabilities."[2]

---

[1] During Operation Desert Storm, for instance, 90 percent of all military equipment and supplies used in the operation were shipped from designated strategic ports in the United States. Frittelli, 2004, p. 6.

[2] Government Accountability Office, *Combating Terrorism, Actions Needed to Improve Force Protection for DoD Deployments Through Domestic Seaports*, Washington, D.C., GAO-03-15, October 2002.

Threat Priorities

In terms of specific maritime threats, piracy and terrorist contingencies involving containerized freight, passenger ferries, and cruise liners are most relevant to U.S. security considerations. Piracy already costs U.S. businesses several millions of dollars a year in lost cargo, delayed trips, damaged vessels, and fraudulent trade, and there is little indication of the situation improving any time soon. In terms of national assets, U.S.-flagged vessels have been frequently targeted, with more than 30 incidents taking place between 2003 and 2005.[3] The figure for 2005 represented a 36 percent rise over 2003's total and was more than double the number of attacks recorded for 2004.[4] Just as problematic are high and ongoing rates of global pirate activity, the effects of which continue to fall disproportionately on the United States simply by virtue of the extensive seaborne trade that the country engages in with industrialized maritime nations.

Terrorist contingencies involving containerized freight have also been consistently highlighted as particularly relevant to U.S. national security. One scenario that has been repeatedly played out because of the volume of (unchecked) containers shipped to U.S. shores is the use of a boxed crate to hide a radiological dispersal device that is then detonated on land.[5] Although the effects of such an attack would depend on the size and sophistication of the dirty bomb employed, it would cause at least localized contamination of the immediate surrounding area (often referred to as "ground shine") and could reasonably

---

[3]   See "Narration of Attacks" sections in International Maritime Bureau, *Piracy and Armed Robbery Against Ships: Annual Report 2003*, London: 2004; International Maritime Bureau, *Piracy and Armed Robbery Against Ships: Annual Report 2004*, London: 2005; and International Maritime Bureau, 2006. Only German, Greek, Japanese, and South Korean carriers suffer from a higher incident rate.

[4]   See International Maritime Bureau, 2006, p. 14.

[5]   More than six million containers enter U.S. ports every year, which accounts for roughly half of the world's present inventory. Of these, only about 10 percent can be expected to have undergone some form of scrutiny. See Sinai, 2004, p. 49; "Maritime Security Measures to Amplify Costs for Shipping," 2003; Block, 2006; Frittelli, 2004, p. 4; and Australian Department of Foreign Affairs and Trade, *Global Issues on Economic Costs of Terrorism*, Canberra: Department of Foreign Affairs and Trade Analytical Unit, April 7, 2003.

be expected to elicit mass public panic of radiological fallout if deaths actually occurred.[6]

Finally, attacks against a rapidly growing cruise industry—in 2004, 78 percent of all passengers vacationing on luxury liners were from North America[7]—need to be taken seriously, not least because they could expose the country to a new form of highly damaging terrorism. A decisive attack against a fully laden passenger ship could be expected to result in a casualty count of several hundred or more.[8] Quite apart from the widespread physical suffering and psychological trauma that this would necessarily engender, it could also have genuinely disruptive political and fiscal effects. Critics, albeit with the benefit of hindsight, would undoubtedly demand to know why the sector was left exposed and why the intelligence services in the relevant flag nation failed to foresee that an attack was imminent. In an age where counterterrorism has emerged as one of the state's most pressing responsibilities, such a reaction could easily precipitate a chain of events that, if not carefully managed, could erode popular perceptions of governing credibility and legitimacy (as it did in Spain following the catastrophic commuter train bombings of 2004).[9]

The economic fallout could be every bit as serious, especially given the highly concentrated character of the cruise business and the fact that this mode of transportation is not integral to an individual's day-to-day

---

[6] Chalk et. al, 2005, p. 34. See also Richardson, 2004, pp. 51–52; Stephen Flynn, "The Neglected Homefront," *Foreign Affairs*, September/October 2004; and Peter Zimmerman, "'Dirty Bombs': The Threat Revisited," *The Back Page*, Vol. 13, No. 3, March 2004.

[7] Over half of this traffic was concentrated in the Caribbean and Alaska. In addition to passengers, two U.S. companies, Royal Caribbean and Carnival, dominate ownership of cruise ships currently in operation. For further details, see William Ebersold, "Industry Overview: Cruise Industry in Figures," *Touch Briefings*, 2004.

[8] An average liner typically caters to at least 200–500 passengers, although several vessels are able to accommodate thousands of guests. While sinking these vessels, which are constructed with safety as a foremost consideration, would be extremely difficult, several less dramatic and more feasible attack options could still result in a large number of fatalities or injuries, including onboard bombings, arson, shootings, and food contamination.

[9] Author interviews with U.K. Customs and Excise, Raytheon International, Glenn Defense Marine Asia, the Maritime Intelligence Group, and Lloyd's, London, Singapore, and Washington, D.C., August and September 2005.

life, travel needs or, indeed, leisure pursuits.[10] As one maritime security analyst in London put it: "If a major cruise liner was hit, the industry will be in big trouble. People just won't sail anymore—either with the company owning the vessel or with one of its [few] competitors."[11] In the United States, this could result in considerable losses, jeopardizing not only approximately $16.2 billion in direct monetary benefit but also the revenue base of major tourist ports—notably Miami, Galveston, Canaveral, New York, Los Angeles, Honolulu, Tampa, Seattle, and (assuming a post-Katrina recovery) New Orleans—as well as some 330,000 full- and part-time jobs.[12]

Principal Security Initiatives Spearheaded by the United States

Reflecting the relevance of a safe and stable oceanic environment to U.S. interests, Washington has been at the forefront of moves to upgrade global maritime security over the last five years. Among the more notable international initiatives that the Bush administration has sponsored are

- The Container Security Initiative (CSI), which involves a series of bilateral, reciprocal accords that, among other things, allow for the forward deployment of U.S. Coast Guard and Border Protection (CBP) officers and their foreign counterparts to prescreen container ships bound for and departing from U.S. shores. As of July 2004, the CSI was operational at 20 overseas ports.[13]

---

[10] See, for instance, ADM James M. Loy, "Seaports, Cruise Ships Vulnerable to Terrorism," guest commentary, PoliticsOL.com, July 28, 2001.

[11] Author interview with Control Risks Group, London, September 2005.

[12] Figures are for 2005, and are derived from International Council of Cruise Lines, "The Cruise Industry 2005 Economic Summary," undated.

[13] U.S. Customs and Border Protection, "Keeping Cargo Safe: Container Security Initiative," undated; Frittelli, 2004, pp. 12–13; Government Accountability Office, *Summary of Challenges Faced in Targeting Oceangoing Cargo Containers for Inspection*, Washington, D.C., GAO-04-557T, March 31, 2004.

- The International Ship and Port Facility Security (ISPS) Code, which was adopted by the International Maritime Organisation at its December 2002 conference and outlines minimum security procedures that all ports and ships above 500 tons must meet to improve overall maritime security. Relevant authorities at the destination terminal can turn away a vessel which does not meet the requirements, or which leaves from a port that does not meet the requirements. Stipulations in the code are based on those embodied in the U.S. Maritime Transport Security Act (MTSA) of 2004.[14]
- The Proliferation Security Initiative (PSI), which aims to combat the proliferation of weapons of mass destruction by sanctioning the right to stop, board, and, if necessary, seize a vessel on the high seas if its is suspected of smuggling chemical, biological, radiological, or nuclear materials. At the time of writing, eleven countries had adopted the PSI: Australia, France, Germany, Italy, Japan, the Netherlands, Poland, Portugal, Spain, the United Kingdom, and the United States.[15]
- The Customs-Trade Partnership Against Terrorism (C-TPAT), which offers international importers expedited processing of cargo if they comply with U.S. CBP guidelines for securing their entire supply chain. Thus far, over 45,000 companies have agreed to participate in C-TPAT.[16]

In addition to these measures, Washington has also been instrumental in instituting regional maritime security initiatives and capac-

---

[14] International Maritime Organisation, "What is the ISPS Code," 2002; Sheppard, 2003, p. 55. The MTSA was passed by the U.S. Congress in 2002. The legislation requires U.S. federal agencies, ports, and vessel owners to take numerous steps to upgrade maritime security, and requires the CBP to develop national and regional plans to secure ocean-based transportation systems. It also requires ports, waterfront terminals, and certain types of vessels to institute their own incident response protocols that must then be submitted to and approved by the Coast Guard. Frittelli, 2004, pp. 14–15.

[15] U.S. Department of State, "State Department Fact Sheet Outlines Proliferation Security Initiative," April 18, 2005; Richardson, 2004, pp. 97–108.

[16] Frittelli, 2004, p. 13.

ity building in areas that are recognized as vital components of American overall counterterrorism strategy. A good example was the 2002 establishment of the Combined Task Force-Horn of Africa, which has a remit to secure the total air, land, and sea space of Djibouti, Ethiopia, Eritrea, Kenya, Somalia, Sudan, and Yemen.[17] The initiative includes an international maritime component, the Combined Task Force-150 (CTF-150), which essentially acts as a counterterrorism patrol unit for the Red Sea, Gulf of Aden, and northwestern Indian Ocean. The CTF-150 has an explicit mandate to deter terrorists from using the maritime environment for planning and conducting attacks, and has conducted tens of thousands of shipping inquiries and hundreds of boardings to this end.[18] Other parts of the globe that have received similar attention include West Africa—especially Nigeria and the wider Gulf of Guinea (which over the coming decade is estimated to account for up to 20 percent of U.S. oil imports)—and the Malacca Straits, particularly the waters that fall under the jurisdiction of the Indonesian government.

Finally, the U.S. has advanced a number of collaborative measures to address transnational maritime security threats. In 2005, for instance, Admiral Michael Mullins proposed a global partnership to tackle issues such as sea-based terrorism and piracy. His idea was to establish common agreement among a "coalition of the willing"[19] on the best ends, ways, and means of facilitating information flows and intelligence exchanges to enhance overall awareness of the maritime domain. Although no definitive agreement had, at the time of writing, been instituted, it is a concept that continues to be actively debated in the United States and by the international shipping community in

---

[17] Clive Schofield, "Horn of Africa Conflicts Threaten U.S. Anti-Terrorism Efforts," *Jane's Intelligence Review*, June 2004, p. 46; Meldrum, 2007, p. 39.

[18] Clive Schofield, "Plaguing the Waves: Rising Piracy Threat off the Horn of Africa," *Jane's Intelligence Review*, July 2007, p. 47.

[19] Mullins actually referred to a "1,000-ship navy"; however, this terminology was changed to mitigate the perception that Washington was advocating the formation of a U.S.-led naval force that would be employed to establish and underwrite U.S. hegemony at sea.

general.[20] Washington has also instituted a so-called Global Fleet Station (GFS) initiative aimed at raising maritime security standards in regions deemed to be of strategic or critical importance. A pilot version of the program, launched in April 2007, involved a six-month deployment of the High Speed Vessel-2 *Swift* to the Caribbean and waters off Central America. The *Swift* served as a single platform for transporting American military instructors to conduct training with regional civil and naval services from seven countries.[21]

A full discussion of the strengths and weaknesses of these measures is beyond the scope of this monograph. However, a few preliminary observations can be made. On the positive side, the initiatives have conferred a degree of transparency to what has, hitherto, been a highly opaque theater. Specifically, they lay the parameters for regulated interstate action in the maritime realm, both by enumerating rules, principles, and attendant responsibilities for international cooperation and, more importantly, by providing a common framework in which to further develop and refine joint policies over the medium to long term. This type of contextual foundation simply did not exist prior to 9/11.[22]

On the negative side, the programs outlined above suffer from three critical shortfalls as presently configured:

- They are limited in scope. The U.S. initiatives are largely confined to a narrow set of like-minded allies, while the ISPS precludes the vast bulk of littoral countries, many of which simply lack the resources to comply fully with its requirements. (Significantly, this has had the inadvertent effect of further increasing the expo-

---

[20] Author interviews with a U.S. Coast Guard official, Asia Pacific Center for Security Studies, Honolulu, August 2007.

[21] For more on GFS and the pilot program in the Caribbean and Central American waters, see MCS1(SW) Cynthia Clark, "Global Fleet Station Deployment Begins," Navy.mil, April 27, 2007.

[22] See, for instance, Stephen Flynn, "On the Record," *Government Executive Magazine,* October 1, 2003.

sure to potential terrorists of what are already vulnerable ports and facilities.)[23]

- The initiatives are largely directed at increasing the security "wall" around commercial seaborne traffic, paying scant regard to contingencies that do not involve containerized cargo (such as ferry bombings) or modalities designed to counter the root source of threats to the oceanic environment, or terrorist organizations themselves.

- With particular reference to the ISPS Code, there is still no definitive means to effectively audit how well extant measures are being implemented by participating states or, indeed, to gauge their overall utility in terms of dockside security. As one maritime analyst summed up with respect to Rotterdam—the world's busiest terminal for oceangoing freight—while the facility is compliant on paper and relatively secure compared to most other international ports, the whole verification procedure remains weak, constituting not much more than "a tick in the box exercise."[24] Moreover, there are presently 43,000 vessels in the global shipping industry that weigh 500 tons or more. This means that roughly 130 ships will need to be certified each day—a task that Lord Westbury, the chief executive officer of Global Marine Security Systems, believes would put a number of smaller companies and ports out of business.[25]

---

[23] Author interviews with IMB, Kuala Lumpur, August 2006.

[24] Author interviews with maritime security analysts, Control Risks Group, Amsterdam, September 2005.

[25] Sheppard, 2003, p. 55.

CHAPTER SIX

Policy Recommendations

The maritime environment will likely remain a favorable theater for armed violence, crime, and terrorism given its expanse, lack of regulation, esoteric character, and general importance as a critical conduit for international trade. There is no quick fix or easy remedy for reducing this openness, and any attempt to institute total security is neither tenable nor desirable. The best that can be hoped for is the rational management of threats within acceptable boundaries. The United States is well placed to facilitate such an effort by virtue of its resources and global influence. At the policy level, there are at least four major contributions that Washington could make, all of which are variously highlighted in the 2005 U.S. *National Strategy for Maritime Security*.[1] First, the United States could help further expand the nascent regime of post-9/11 maritime security, both in terms of pressing littoral states to sign multilateral protocols and instituting effective structures for measuring and ensuring compliance with their stipulations. To add credence to this effort, the United States should immediately ratify UNCLOS, one of the key international legal instruments governing sovereign rights at sea.[2] Second, the United States could inform the

---

[1] For a full version of this document see The White House, *The National Strategy for Maritime Security*, Washington, D.C., September 2005.

[2] The United States has not ratified UNCLOS largely due to the objections of a small number of senators who oppose the Convention on the grounds that it runs counter to U.S. national interests and undercuts the country's sovereignty. There has, however, been strong domestic pressure to ratify the agreement as part of the overall effort to institutionalize a more thorough regime of maritime security post-9/11, with President Bush specifically rais-

parameters of bilateral and multilateral maritime security collaboration by conducting regular and rigorous threat assessments that are aimed at delineating high probability risk scenarios and quantifying their costs. Third, the United States could help redefine mandates of existing multilateral security and defense arrangements to allow them to play a more effective and inclusive role in countering maritime (and other transnational) threats. Fourth, the United States could encourage the commercial maritime industry to make greater use of enabling communication and defensive technologies and accept a greater degree of overall transparency in its underlying corporate structures.

In more specific terms, U.S. funds and support could be usefully directed at

1. Boosting the coastal monitoring and interdiction capabilities of states in areas of strategic maritime importance or endemic pirate activity through the provision of surveillance assets, training, and technical support.[3] The GFS initiative described above may be particularly relevant in this regard.

2. Actively encouraging the IMB's anti-piracy center in Malaysia—the international system's main non-governmental organization for monitoring manifestations of armed violence at sea— to expand its current (limited) reporting role to one that has a more explicit investigative function.[4]

---

ing the issue in March 2007. Author interview, United Coast Guard official, Asia Pacific Center for Security Studies, Honolulu, August 2007.

[3] Because many littoral states in need of coastal surveillance support also suffer from high rates of corruption (e.g., Nigeria, the Philippines, Indonesia, Thailand, Kenya), the provision of material, as opposed to financial, assistance is generally regarded as preferable.

[4] Since its initial inception in 1992, the IMB's reporting center in Kuala Lumpur has played an integral role in identifying operational and geographic patterns of armed violence at sea and in transmitting real-time warnings and updates to mariners traveling in or near pirate "hot spots." The center has also served as a central conduit for information exchange between shipping associations and companies located in Asia, Africa, Europe, and the Middle East. A new Information Sharing Center established in Singapore in 2006 has a similar mandate, but it is not yet apparent whether this institution is meant to supplement or supplant the IMB body.

3. Augmenting port security management by underwriting diligent screening protocols and systems aimed at vetting the "bona fides" of arriving and departing vessels, the crews that staff these ships, and the companies that own and run them.[5]

4. Sponsoring public-private sector partnerships for further developing monitoring and protective initiatives such as ShipLoc (an inexpensive satellite tracking system that has been endorsed by the IMB),[6] Secure-Ship (a non-lethal perimeter electric fence designed to prevent unauthorized boardings),[7] and so-called "smart" containers that can emit warnings if their contents are disturbed after being sealed.

5. Promoting greater openness in the international maritime industry as a whole by, for example, offering incentives aimed at encouraging shipping companies to register their vessels through traditional flag states (as opposed to FoCs) and to accept a fundamentally more transparent ownership disclosure system.[8] Possible inducements might include prioritization for offshore anchor releases, expedited freight clearance procedures, and cheaper docking fees.

---

[5] The general issue of port security management has also been raised with respect to the United States. In 2006, this became an especially hot topic after Dubai Ports World, a company owned and operated out of the United Arab Emirates, purchased the Peninsular and Oriental Steam Navigation Company of the United Kingdom, giving it the right to oversee major operations at terminals in New York, New Jersey, Philadelphia, Baltimore, New Orleans, and Miami. Although the takeover was approved, Dubai Ports eventually pulled out of the deal after members of Congress raised concern over the potential ramifications it might have for port security given the United Arab Emirates' alleged role in funding the al Qaeda network. For more on the incident, see Neil King and Greg Hitt, "Dubai Ports World Sells U.S. Assets," *The Wall Street Journal*, December 11, 2006.

[6] ShipLoc allows shipping companies to monitor the exact location of their vessels anywhere in the world on a 24/7, 365-day per year basis via Internet access. For more on the system, see "ShipLoc," homepage, undated.

[7] For further details on this initiative, see Secure Marine, "Secure-Ship," Web page, 2002.

[8] For analysis of the shipping industry's reluctance to accept greater transparency in terms of vessel ownership and operation, see Meldrum, 2007, pp. 36–39.

In whatever capacity the United States chooses to support or promote anti-piracy and terrorism measures, coordinating initiatives with other concerned littoral states and international organizations needs to be emphasized as much as possible.[9] Not only will this allow Washington to offset some of the cost of its assistance programs, it would also help to reduce latent perceptions that the general issue of maritime security is exclusively tied to U.S. strategic priorities.[10] Just as importantly, working with or through partner countries and organizations will give the U.S. government greater flexibility and latitude in developing indigenous capabilities in sensitive areas and regions where strictly unilateral action would be difficult (or impossible)—a potential reality in many parts of the Middle East, Persian Gulf, and South and Southeast Asia.

---

[9]   An example of local multilateral cooperation is the "Eye in the Sky" initiative inaugurated in 2005 among Malaysia, Indonesia, Singapore, and Thailand. The idea—which reportedly developed in reaction to Lloyds' designation of the SLOC as an AER risk—ostensibly aims to provide limited airborne surveillance over the Malacca Straits and builds off the earlier Malaysia-Singapore-Indonesia (MASLINDO) accord. Under the initiative, each participating country will make two planes available, and commit to flying two sorties a week over the Straits. Therefore, for every seven days there will be at least 16 hours of continual coverage over the waterway. The Philippines has expressed active interest in future iterations of the agreement, and both Japan and Australia have pledged to provide additional resources so that a more extensive system of surveillance can evolve. Author interview, IMB, Kuala Lumpur, August 2006.

[10]   In 2004, for instance, various entities suggested that the U.S. Navy might provide armed escorts for ships transiting the Malacca Straits. Indonesia and Malaysia, however, vigorously rejected this idea on the grounds that it would represent a wholly unjustified expansion of U.S. influence in areas close to their territorial waters. Even Singapore expressed reservations about the strategic and political implications of a concerted American presence in the Straits. Comments made during the International Cooperation in the War Against Terror in the Asia-Pacific Region with a Special Emphasis on the Malacca Straits Conference, Mississippi State University, March 8–9, 2006.

Selected High-Profile Maritime Terrorist Incidents, 1961–2004

Table A.1
Selected High-Profile Maritime Terrorist Incidents, 1961–2004

Incident	Group	Deaths	Remarks
Hijacking of Santa Maria (1961)	Portuguese and Spanish rebels	0	The Santa Maria, a 21,000-ton cruise ship owned by Companhia Colonial of Lisbon, was hijacked by a group of 70 men led by Captain Henriques Galvao (a Portuguese political exile) to bring global attention to the Estado Novo in Portugal and a related fascist regime in Spain. The vessel was on a holiday cruise in the southern Caribbean and its more than 600 passengers were held for 11 days before Galvao formally surrendered to the Brazilian Navy. The incident constitutes the first modern-day hijack at sea.[a]
Use of a Cypriot-registered coaster, Claudia, to transport weapons to Ireland (1973)	Provisional Irish Republican Army	0	Claudia was intercepted by the Irish Navy while attempting to land a consignment of weapons intended for the Provisional Irish Republican Army (PIRA). On board were five tons of munitions that included 250 Soviet-made assault rifles, pistols, mines, grenades, and explosives. The vessel was owned by Gunther Leinhauser, a West German arms dealer who said that PIRA had given him a "shopping list" of required material and that the "order" had been filled by Libya.[b]
Hijacking of Achille Lauro (1985)	Palestine Liberation Front	1	The Achille Lauro, a cruise ship, was hijacked in an attempt to coerce the release of 50 Palestinians being held in Israel. The perpetrators were eventually detained in Sicily. One person was killed in the incident: Leon Kling-Hoffer, a wheelchair-bound German tourist, was killed and then pushed overboard.[c]
Targeting of cruise ships on the Nile River (1992–1994)	Al-Gama'a al-Islamyya	0	The group targeted at least four cruise ships during these two years as part of its general effort to undermine the Egyptian tourist sector (a key contributor to the country's economy).[d]

Table A.1—Continued

Incident	Group	Deaths	Remarks
Hijacking of a Turkish passenger ferry in the Black Sea (1996)	Chechen rebels	0	Nine rebel gunmen held 255 passengers hostage for four days during which they threatened to blow up the captured ferry in order to bring international attention to the Chechen cause. The abductors eventually sailed the vessel back to Istanbul, where they surrendered.[e]
Suicide bombing of the USS *Cole* (2000)	Al Qaeda	17	The bombing took place while the *Cole* was refueling at the Port of Aden. The assault involved 600 pounds of C4 explosives that were packed into the hull of a suicide attack skiff. Seventeen U.S. sailors and two terrorists were killed, and another 39 sailors were injured.[f]
Suicide bombing of the M/V *Limburg* (2002)[g]	Al Qaeda	3	The attack involved a small, fiberglass boat packed with 100–200 kg of TNT that was rammed into the tanker as it prepared to begin a pilot-assisted approach to the Ash Shihr Terminal off the coast of Yemen. The *Limburg* was lifting 297,000 barrels of crude oil at the time of the strike, an estimated 50,000 of which spilled into the waters surrounding the stricken vessel. One crewman and two terrorists were killed.[h]
Use of the *Karine A* to transport weapons for anti-Israeli strikes (2002)	Palestinian Authority	0	The *Karine A*, a 4,000-ton freighter, was seized in the Red Sea on January 3, 2002. The vessel was carrying a wide assortment of Russian and Iranian munitions, including Katyusha rockets (with a range of 20 km), antitank missiles, long-range mortar bombs, mines, sniper rifles, ammunition, and more than two tons of high explosives. The weapons consignment, estimated at $100 million, was linked directly to Yassir Arafat and was allegedly to be used for attacks against Jewish targets in Israel and the Occupied Territories.[i]

Table A.1—Continued

Incident	Group	Deaths	Remarks
Hijacking of the M/V *Penrider*, a fully laden oil tanker en route from Singapore to Penang (2003)	Gerakan Aceh Merdeka	0	The M/V *Penrider*, a fully-laden oil tanker, was seized while en route from Singapore to Penang in northern Malaysia. The incident was one of the few cases where Gerakan Aceh Merdeka openly took responsibility for a maritime attack (the group has been linked to several hijackings and maritime assaults off the coast of Aceh). The group's three hostages (the master, chief engineer, and second engineer) were released upon payment of a $52,000 ransom.[j]
Use of the *Abu Hassan* to transport weapons and training manuals to assist militant strikes in Israel (2003)	Lebanese Hezbollah	0	The owner of the *Abu Hassan*, an Egyptian-registered fishing trawler, was recruited by Hezbollah and specifically trained to carry out maritime support missions. The vessel, which Israeli Navy commandos intercepted 35 nautical miles off the coast of Haifa, was being used to ferry a complex weapons and logistics consignment consisting of fuses for 122-mm Qassam rockets, electronic time-delay fuses, a training video for carrying out suicide missions, and two sets of CD-ROMs containing detailed bomb-making information.[k]
Attacks against the Khor al-Amaya and Al-Basra offshore oil terminals in Iraq (2004)	Jamaat al-Tawhid (Unity and Jihad Group)	3	The attacks were claimed by Abu Musab al-Zarqawi as a follow up to the 2000 *Cole* and 2002 *Limburg* strikes. The operation led to the closure of both facilities at an estimated cost of $40 million and are generally considered to be part of a concerted strategy aimed at the economic destabilization of the post-Hussein administration in Baghdad.[l]

Table A.1—Continued

Incident	Group	Deaths	Remarks
Bombing of the Philippine *SuperFerry 14* (2004)	Abu Sayyaf, combined with elements from the Rajah Soliaman Movement and Jemaah Islamyya	116	The attack involved 20 sticks of dynamite that were planted in a hollowed-out television set. The bomb set off a fire that rapidly spread throughout the ship due to the lack of an effective sprinkler system. The incident has been listed as the most destructive act of terrorism in maritime history and the fourth most serious attack since 9/11.[m]
Suicide attacks against the Port of Ashdod in Israel (2004)	Hamas, al-Aqsa Martyr's Brigade	10	The attack, which was jointly executed by a combined Hamas/al-Aqsa Martyr's Brigade team, left ten people dead and involved two Palestinian terrorists who had been smuggled to the terminal inside a commercial container four hours before the operation. Some speculate that al Qaeda assisted with the logistics of the strike.[n]

SOURCE: Adapted from Greenberg et al., 2006, pp. 20–24.

[a] Jenkins et al., 1986, p. 69. The hijacking was also known as "Operation Dulcinea" by the hijackers.

[b] Wilkinson, 1986, pp. 39.

[c] The Palestine Liberation Front's original intention was to seize the *Achille Lauro* and then ram the vessel into an Israeli oil terminal at Ashod. However, the attack was discovered before this operation could be put into effect, forcing a change in plan. Author interview with security and terrorism analyst, Monterrey, California, November 2006.

[d] Sinai, 2004, p. 50; John Sitilides, "US Strikes Expose Emerging Regional Threats," *The HR-Net Forum: The Washington Monitor,* August 28, 1998.

[e] Sinai, 2004, p. 50; Stilides, 1998; Koknar, 2005; "Hostage Taking Action by Pro-Chechen Rebels Impairs Turkey's Image," *People's Daily* (China), April 24, 2001.

Table A.1—Continued

f For more on this incident, see Raphael Perl, *Terrorist Attack on the USS Cole: Background and Issues for Congress*, Washington, D.C.: Congressional Research Service, RS20721, January 30, 2001. Although it was directed against a warship, this attack has been designated a terrorist strike because the *Cole* was no actively deployed at the time of the bombing.

g The *M/V Limburg* has since been renamed and now operates under the designation *M/V Maritime Jewel*.

h Herbert-Burns, 2005, p. 164; Valencia, 2005b, p. 84; Ho, 2003; "Investigators to Board Yemen tanker," *BBC Online News*, October 9, 2002.

i "IDF Seizes PA Weapons Ship," Jewish Virtual Library, January 4, 2002.

j Herbert-Burns, 2005, pp. 167–168; Kate McGeown, "Aceh Rebels Blamed for Piracy," *BBC Online News*, September 8, 2003; International Maritime Organisation, *Reports on Acts of Piracy and Armed Robbery Against Ships*, London: September 4, 2003.

k Herbert-Burns, 2005, p. 166.

l Mirelle Warouw, "The Threat Against Maritime Assets: A Review of Historical Cases, Operational Patterns and Indicators," unpublished paper, Institute of Defense and Strategic Studies, Singapore, 2005, p. 12. Also see Koknar, 2005.

m Peter Chalk, "The SuperFerry 14 Bombing, 2004," *Jane's Terrorism and Insurgency Center*, Case Study No. 5, 2006.

n Koknar, 2005.

References

ShipLoc, homepage, undated. As of January 27, 2008:
http://www.shiploc.com/

Abyankar, Jayant, "Phantom Ships," in Ellen (1997).

————, "Piracy and Ship Robbery: A Growing Menace," in Ahmad and Ogawa (2001).

Ahmad, Hamzah and Akira Ogawa, eds., *Combating Piracy and Ship Robbery*, Tokyo: Okazaki Institute, 2001.

"Al Qaeda Has Multi Faceted Marine Strategy," Agence France Press, January 20, 2003.

Australian Department of Foreign Affairs and Trade, *Global Issues on Economic Costs of Terrorism*, Canberra: Department of Foreign Affairs and Trade Analytical Unit, April 7, 2003.

Banaloi, Rommel, "Maritime Terrorism in Southeast Asia," *Naval War College Review*, Vol. 58, No. 4, Autumn 2005.

Bateman, Sam, and Stephen Bates, eds., *Calming the Waters: Initiatives for Asia-Pacific Maritime Cooperation*, Canberra: Strategic and Defence Studies Centre, 1996.

Beckman, Robert, Carl Grundy-Warr, and Vivian Forbes, "Acts of Piracy in the Malacca Straits," *Maritime Briefing*, Vol. 1, No. 4, 1994.

Block, Robert, "Security Gaps Already Plague Ports," *The Wall Street Journal*, February 23, 2006.

Boutwell, Jeffrey, and Michael T. Klare, eds., *Lethal Commerce: The Global Trade in Small Arms and Light Weapons*, Cambridge, Mass.: American Academy of Sciences, 1995.

Chaikin, Greg, "Piracy in Asia: International Cooperation and Japan's Role," in Johnson and Valencia (2005).

Chalk, Peter, *West European Terrorism and Counter-Terrorism: The Evolving Dynamic*, London: MacMillan, 1996.

————, *Non-Military Security and Global Order: The Impact of Extremism, Violence and Chaos on National and International Security*, London: Macmillan, 2000.

————, "The SuperFerry 14 Bombing, 2004," *Jane's Terrorism and Insurgency Center*, Case Study No. 5, 2006.

Chalk, Peter, Bruce Hoffman, Robert T. Reville, and Anna-Britt Kasupski, *Trends in Terrorism: Threats to the United States and the Future of the Terrorism Risk Insurance Act*, Santa Monica, Calif.: RAND Corporation, MG-393-CTRMP, 2005. As of November 27, 2007:
http://www.rand.org/pubs/monographs/MG393/

Commercial Crime Services, "International Maritime Bureau—Overview," Web page, 2007. As of December 18, 2007:
http://www.icc-ccs.org/imb/overview.php

Davis, Anthony, "Tracing the Dynamics of the Illicit Arms Trade," *Jane's Intelligence Review*, September 2003.

Dixon, Lloyd, and Robert T. Reville, "National Security and Compensation Policy for Terrorism Losses," in *Catastrophic Risks and Insurance: Policy Issues in Insurance*, Paris: Organisation for Economic Co-operation and Development, 2006.

Dixon, Lloyd, and Rachel Kaganoff Stern, *Compensation for Losses from the 9/11 Attacks*, Santa Monica, Calif.: RAND Corporation, MG-264-ICJ, 2004. As of November 27, 2007:
http://www.rand.org/pubs/monographs/MG264/

Djalal, Hasjim, "Combating Piracy: Co-operation, Needs, Efforts and Challenges," in Johnson and Valencia (2005).

Eavis, Paul, "Awash with Light Weapons," *The World Today*, April 1999.

Ebersold, William, "Industry Overview: Cruise Industry in Figures," *Touch Briefings*, 2004. As of November 9, 2005:
http://www.touchbriefings.com/pdf/858/ebersold.pdf

Ellen, Eric, ed., *Violence at Sea*, Paris: International Chamber of Commerce, 1986.

————, ed., *Shipping at Risk*, London: International Chamber of Commerce, 1997.

Flynn, Stephen, "On the Record," *Government Executive Magazine*, October 1, 2003.

————, "The Neglected Homefront," *Foreign Affairs*, September/October, 2004.

"For Those in Peril on the Sea," *The Economist*, August 9, 1997.

Fritelli, John, *Port and Maritime Security: Background and Issues for Congress*, Washington, D.C.: Congressional Research Service, December 30, 2004.

Furdson, Edward, "Sea Piracy—or Maritime Mugging?" *INTERSEC*, Vol. 6, No. 5, May 1996.

Government Accountability Office, *Combating Terrorism, Actions Needed to Improve Force Protection for DoD Deployments Through Domestic Seaports*, Washington, D.C., GAO-03-15, October 2002.

———, *Summary of Challenges Faced in Targeting Oceangoing Cargo Containers for Inspection*, Washington, D.C., GAO-04-557T, March 31, 2004.

Clark, MCS1(SW) Cynthia, "Global Fleet Station Deployment Begins," Navy.mil, April 27, 2007. As of November 29, 2007:
http://www.navy.mil/search/display.asp?story_id=29095

Greenberg, Michael, Peter Chalk, Henry Willis, Ivan Khilko, and David Ortiz, *Maritime Terrorism: Risk and Liability*, Santa Monica, Calif.: RAND Corporation, MG-520-CTRMP, 2006. As of November 27, 2007:
http://www.rand.org/pubs/monographs/MG520/

Herbert-Burns, Rupert, "Terrorism in the Early 21st Century Maritime Domain," in Ho and Raymond (2005).

Ho, Joshua, "Security of Sea-Lanes in Southeast Asia," unpublished paper, Indian Observer Research Foundation Workshop on Maritime Counterterrorism, New Delhi, November 29–30, 2004.

Ho, Joshua, and Catherine Zara Raymond, eds., *The Best of Times, the Worst of Times: Maritime Security in the Asia-Pacific*, Singapore: World Scientific Publishing, 2005.

Ho, Vivian, "No Let Down in Global Pirate Attacks by Pirates," Kyodo News Service, July 24, 2003.

"Hostage Taking Action by Pro-Chechen Rebels Impairs Turkey's Image," *People's Daily* (China), April 24, 2001.

Hunt, Matthew, "Bleed to Bankruptcy," *Jane's Intelligence Review*, January 2007.

"IDF Seizes PA Weapons Ship," Jewish Virtual Library, January 4, 2002. As of November 28, 2007:
http://www.jewishvirtuallibrary.org/jsource/Peace/paship.html

International Council of Cruise Lines, "The Cruise Industry 2005 Economic Summary," undated. As of November 29, 2007:
http://www.iccl.org/resources/2005_econ_summary.pdf

International Maritime Bureau, *Piracy and Armed Robbery Against Ships: Special Report*, London: International Chamber of Commerce, 1997.

————, *Piracy and Armed Robbery Against Ships: Annual Report 2003*, London, 2004.

————, *Piracy and Armed Robbery Against Ships: Annual Report 2004*, London, 2005.

————, *Piracy and Armed Robbery Against Ships: Report for the Period 1 January— 30 September 2005*, London, November 8, 2005.

————, *Piracy and Armed Robbery Against Ships: Annual Report 2005*, London, 2006.

————, *Piracy and Armed Robbery Against Ships: Annual Report, 2006*, London, 2007.

International Maritime Organisation, "What is the ISPS Code," 2002. As of November 29, 2007:
http://www.imo.org/TCD/mainframe.asp?topic_id=897#what

————, *Reports on Acts of Piracy and Armed Robbery Against Ships*, London, September 4, 2003.

The International Monetary Fund, *World Economic Outlook*, Washington, D.C., 1991.

"Investigators to Board Yemen Tanker," *BBC Online News*, October 9, 2002. As of August 20, 2006:
http://news.bbc.co.uk/1/hi/world/middle_east/2312739.stm

Jehl, Douglas, and David Johnson, "In Video Message, bin Laden Issues Warning to U.S." *The New York Times*, October 30, 2004.

Jenkins, Brian, Bonnie Cordes, Karen Gardela, and Geraldine Petty, "A Chronology of Terrorist Attacks and Other Criminal Actions Against Maritime Targets," in Ellen (1986).

Johnson, Derek, Erika Pladdet, and Mark Valencia, "Research on Southeast Asian Piracy," in Johnson and Valencia (2005).

Johnson, Derek, and Mark Valencia, eds., *Piracy in Southeast Asia*, Singapore: Institute of Southeast Asian Studies, 2005.

Karp, Aaron, "Small Arms—The New Major Weapons, in Boutwell and Klare (1995).

Kaldor, Mary, and Basker Vashee, eds., *New Wars: Restructuring the Global Military Sector*, London: Pinter, 1997.

King, Neil, and Greg Hitt, "Dubai Ports World Sells U.S. Assets," *The Wall Street Journal*, December 11, 2006.

Klare, Michael T., "An Avalanche of Guns: Light Weapons Trafficking and Armed Conflict in the Post-Cold War Era," in Kaldor and Vashee (1997).

————, "The Kalashnikov Age," *Bulletin of the Atomic Scientists*, Vol. 55, No. 1, January/February 1999.

Koknar, Ali, "Maritime Terrorism: A New Challenge for NATO," *Energy Security*, January 24, 2005. As of December 8, 2005:
http://www.iags.org/n0124051.htm

Latham, Andrew, "The Light Weapons Problem: Causes, Consequences and Policy Options," in Latham (1996).

————, ed., *Multilateral Approaches to Non-Proliferation: Proceedings of the 4th Canadian Non-Proliferation Workshop*, Toronto: Centre for International and Security Studies, 1996.

Loy, ADM James M., "Seaports, Cruise Ships Vulnerable to Terrorism," guest commentary, PoliticsOL.com, July 28, 2001. As of November 7, 2005:
http://www.politicalsol.com/guest-commentaries/2001-07-28.html

"Maritime Security Measures to Amplify Costs for Shipping," *Transport Security World*, July 29, 2003.

McGeown, Kate, "Aceh Rebels Blamed for Piracy," *BBC Online News*, September 8, 2003. As of May 1, 2006:
http://news.bbc.co.uk/1/hi/world/asia-pacific/3090136.stm

Meldrum, Catherine, "Murky Waters: Financing Maritime Terrorism and Crime," *Jane's Intelligence Review*, June 2007.

Mukundan, P., "The Scourge of Piracy in Southeast Asia: Can Any Improvements be Expected in the Future?" in Johnson and Valencia (2005).

Murphy, Martin, "Maritime Terrorism: Threat in Context," *Jane's Intelligence Review*, February 2006.

————, *Contemporary Piracy and Maritime Terrorism: The Threat to International Security*, London: International Institute for Strategic Studies, Adelphi Paper 338, 2007.

NUMAST Telegraph, Vol. 25, No. 7, Piracy Supplement, July 1992.

Ong, Graham, "Ships Can Be Dangerous Too: Coupling Piracy and Terrorism in Southeast Asia's Maritime Security Framework," in Johnson and Valencia (2005).

Organisation for Economic Co-operation and Development, *Security in Maritime Transport: Risk Factors and Economic Impact*, Paris: July 2003. As of August 18, 2006:
http://www.oecd.org/dataoecd/19/61/18521672.pdf

————, *Report on Security in Maritime Transport: Risk Factors and Economic Impact*, Paris, July 2003.

Percival, Bronson, *Indonesia and the United States: Shared Interests in Maritime Security*, Washington, D.C.: United States-Indonesia Society, June 2005.

Perl, Raphael, *Terrorist Attack on the USS Cole: Background and Issues for Congress*, Washington, D.C., Congressional Research Service, RS20721, January 30, 2001.

Prakash, Metaparti, "Maritime Terrorism: Threats to Port and Container Security and Scope for Regional Co-operation," paper presented at the 12th Meeting of the Council for Security Cooperation in the Asia Pacific Working Group on Maritime Co-operation, Singapore, December 10–11, 2002.

Pugh, Michael, "Piracy and Armed Robbery at Sea: Problems and Remedies," *Low Intensity Conflict and Law Enforcement*, Vol. 2, No. 1, 1993.

Quentin, Sophia, "Shipping Activities: Targets of Maritime Terrorism," *MIRMAL*, Vol. 2, January 20, 2003. As of October 18, 2005:
http://www.derechomaritimo.info/pagina/mater.htm

Raymond, Catherine Zara, " Maritime Terrorism, A Risk Assessment: The Australian Example," in Ho and Raymond (2005).

Richardson, Michael, *A Time Bomb for Global Trade*, Singapore: Institute of Southeast Asian Studies, 2004.

Schofield, Clive, "Horn of Africa Conflicts Threaten US Anti-Terrorism Efforts," *Jane's Intelligence Review*, June 2004.

———, "Plaguing the Waves: Rising Piracy Threat off the Horn of Africa," *Jane's Intelligence Review*, July 2007.

Secure Marine, "Secure-Ship," Web page, 2002. As of January 30, 2008:
http://www.secure-marine.com/ship_intro.htm

"Security Fears Keep Israeli Ships from Turkey," *The New York Times*, August 9, 2005.

Sezer, Murad, "Turkish Court Charges Suspected al-Qaeda Militant," Associated Press, August 10, 2005.

Sheppard, Ben, "Maritime Security Measures," *Jane's Intelligence Review*, March 2003.

Sinai, Joshua, "Future Trends in Worldwide Maritime Terrorism," *Connections: The Quarterly Journal*, Vol. 3, No. 1, March 2004.

Smith, Chris, "Light Weapons Proliferation: A Global Survey," *Jane's Intelligence Review*, July 1999.

Stilides, John, "US Strikes Expose Emerging Regional Threats," *The HR-Net Forum: The Washington Monitor*, August 28, 1998. As of May 1, 2006:
http://www.hri.org/forum/intpol/wm.98-08-28.html

Takita, Kazuo and Bob Couttie, "ASEAN Pressured to Act Against Pirates," *Lloyd's List*, May 29, 1992.

"Terrorism and the Warfare of the Weak," *The Guardian*, October 27, 1993.

U.S. Customs and Border Protection, "Keeping Cargo Safe: Container Security Initiative," undated. As of October 26, 2006:
http://www.cbp.gov/xp/cgov/border_security/international_activities/csi/

U.S. Department of State, "State Department Fact Sheet Outlines Proliferation Security Initiative," April 18, 2005. As of November 29, 2007:
http://usinfo.state.gov/is/Archive/2005/Apr/18-12261.htm

Valencia, Mark, "Piracy and Politics in Southeast Asia," 2005a, in Johnson and Valencia (2005).

————, "Piracy and Terrorism in Southeast Asia: Similarities, Differences and their Implications," 2005b, in Johnson and Valencia (2005).

Warouw, Mirelle, "The Threat Against Maritime Assets: A Review of Historical Cases, Operational Patterns and Indicators," unpublished paper, Institute of Defense and Strategic Studies, Singapore, 2005.

Watkins, Eric, "Security—Al'Qa'eda Suspect Admits Role in Limburg," *Lloyd's List*, January 21, 2003.

Weeks, Stanley, "Law and Order at Sea: Pacific Cooperation in Dealing with Piracy, Drugs and Illegal Migration," in Bateman and Bates (1996).

The White House, *National Strategy for Maritime Security*, Washington, D.C.: September 2005. As of August 4, 2005:
http://www.whitehouse.gov/homeland/4844-nsms.pdf

Wilkinson, Paul, "Terrorism and the Maritime Environment," in Ellen (1986).

World Trade Organization, *International Trade Statistics 2006*, Table 1.3, November 2006. As of July 28, 2007:
http://www.wto.org/english/res_e/statis_e/its2006_e/its06_toc_e.htm

Young, Adam and Mark Valencia, "Piracy and Terrorism Threats Overlap," *The Washington Times*, July 7, 2003.

Young, Adam, "Conflation of Piracy and Terrorism in Southeast Asia: Rectitude and Utility," *Contemporary Southeast Asia*, Vol. 25, No. 2, August 2003.

Zimmerman, Peter, "'Dirty Bombs': The Threat Revisited," *The Back Page*, Vol. 13, No. 3, March 2004.